Hasidic Warsaw

This volume of YIVO's Yiddish Voices Series was prepared for publication with generous support from the family of Harriet R. Yassky

YIVO Institute for Jewish Research

YIDDISH VOICES

Series Editors

Yiddish Voices is an exciting new series of translated works that connects today's readers with literature that reflects the Eastern European Jewish experience, in its full range of authors, genres, and subject matter.

Published in partnership with the YIVO Institute for Jewish Research, each volume presents a rich and engaging literary work in English translation with a well-matched historian's introduction, one that is both erudite and readable. In Yiddish, the word "Yiddish" means both "Yiddish" and "Jewish"; likewise, the *Yiddish Voices* series includes translated works from an array of languages—sometimes Yiddish, but at other times Polish, Russian, or Hebrew, among others. The series thus captures both the Yiddish and the Yiddish-inflected, the Yiddish voices and Ashkenazi experiences as they came to be embedded in other cultural spheres.

Expertly curated by Alyssa Quint and Elissa Bemporad, the series is organized to showcase first-time translations of enduring texts in Yiddish from which arise topics and themes that have powerful resonance today.

Editorial Advisory Board

Published Titles

Three Yiddish Plays by Women: Female Jewish Perspectives, 1880–1920, ed. Alyssa Quint
The Mother of Yiddish Theatre: Memoirs of Esther-Rokhl Kaminska, ed. and trans. Mikhl Yashinsky
The Destruction of Dubova: Chronicle of a Dead City, by Rokhl Faygnberg, ed. Elissa Bemporad
Hasidic Warsaw: Reb Zalmen and the Aleksander Shtibl, by Yechiel Hofer, ed. and trans. Jonathan Boyarin
Mississippi: A Yiddish Play about the Scottsboro Affair, by Leib Malach, ed. Alyssa Quint

Upcoming Titles

The Diary of Jula Wald, 1918–24, ed. Glenn Dynner
My Mother's Silence: Confronting the Holocaust and its Memory, by Lizzie Doron, ed. Philip Hollander
Women of the Ghetto: A Novella, by Chaim Grade, ed. David Fishman
Glatt Kosher: The Life of Shimon Dzigan, ed. Diego Rotman

Hasidic Warsaw

Reb Zalmen and the Aleksander Shtibl

BY YECHIEL HOFER

EDITED AND TRANSLATED BY JONATHAN BOYARIN

BLOOMSBURY ACADEMIC
LONDON • NEW YORK • OXFORD • NEW DELHI • SYDNEY

BLOOMSBURY ACADEMIC
Bloomsbury Publishing Plc, 50 Bedford Square, London, WC1B 3DP, UK
Bloomsbury Publishing Inc, 1359 Broadway, New York, NY 10018, USA
Bloomsbury Publishing Ireland, 29 Earlsfort Terrace,
Dublin 2, D02 AY28, Ireland

BLOOMSBURY, BLOOMSBURY ACADEMIC and the Diana logo are trademarks of Bloomsbury Publishing Plc

First published in Great Britain 2026

Series cover design by Julian Schmidt and Julia Steinman
Cover image: Hasidic men and boys walking back from shul in Warsaw, detail, 1929 © Photograph by Alter Kacyzne. Courtesy of the Archives of the YIVO Institute for Jewish Research, New York/Forward Association, New York.

A catalogue record for this book is available from the British Library.

A catalog record for this book is available from the Library of Congress.

ISBN: HB: 978-1-3505-1740-0
PB: 978-1-3505-1737-0
ePDF: 978-1-3505-1738-7
eBook: 978-1-3505-1736-3

Typeset by RefineCatch Limited, Bungay, Suffolk
Printed and bound in Great Britain

CONTENTS

LIST OF ILLUSTRATIONS

CONTRIBUTOR

Jonathan Boyarin's work centers on Jewish communities and on the dynamics of Jewish culture, memory, and identity. He has investigated these fields in a range of ethnographic projects set in Paris, Jerusalem, and the Lower East Side of New York City. Much of his work is in interdisciplinary critical theory, almost always from the perspective of modern Jewish politics and experience. He has extended these interests into comparative work on diaspora, the politics of time and space, and the ethnography of reading. His books include *From a Ruined Garden: The Memorial Books of Polish Jewry* (with Jack Kugelmass, 1998, 2nd edition), *Mornings at the Stanton Street Shul: A Lower East Side Summer* (2011), *Jewish Families* (2013), and *Yeshiva Days: Learning on the Lower East Side* (2020). Previous translations from Yiddish include *A Fire Burns in Kotsk* by Menashe Unger (2013).

FIGURE 1 *The Aleksander Rebbe (center) with his children and retinue. Taken at the summer resort in Ciechocinek, Poland, c. 1926. Photograph by Menachem Kipnis. Courtesy of the Archives of the YIVO Institute for Jewish Research, New York.*

FIGURE 2 *The young heir to the Aleksander Hasidic dynasty at the summer resort in Ciechocinek, Poland, 1926. The photographer wrote, "He strolls about the resort accompanied by three Hasidim and stands at attention if one asks to photograph him." Photograph by Menachem Kipnis. Courtesy of the Archives of the YIVO Institute for Jewish Research, New York/Forward Association, New York.*

FIGURE 3 *Street in Falenice, near Warsaw, 1923. Photograph by Alter Kacyzne. Courtesy of the Archives of the YIVO Institute for Jewish Research, New York/Forward Association, New York.*

FIGURE 4 *Hasidic men and boys walking back from shul in Warsaw, 1929. Photograph by Alter Kacyzne. Courtesy of the Archives of the YIVO Institute for Jewish Research, New York/Forward Association, New York.*

FIGURE 5 *The photographer wrote on the back: "The lively multitudes in the Hala Mirowska Square, Warsaw, before* yontef, *1920s." Photograph by Alter Kacyzne. Courtesy of the Archives of the YIVO Institute for Jewish Research, New York/Forward Association, New York.*

Introduction

Jonathan Boyarin

The Israeli writer Yechiel Hofer, born in Warsaw in the years shortly before World War I, was a scion of a wealthy Hasidic family. He trained as a physician before World War II and began his literary career in Polish. His several Yiddish volumes consist largely of works drawing heavily on memory, although some are labeled as novels and others not. While a few of his books were translated into Hebrew, none until now have been published in English. *Reb Zalmen* is of particular interest for its depiction of Hasidic life in early twentieth-century Warsaw.

Hofer's father was a follower of the Aleksander Rebbe, and as a youngster Hofer was intimately familiar with the headquarters of that Rebbe's followers in Warsaw, a place known as the Aleksander *shtibl*. It was one of numerous *shtiblekh* in the Jewish quarter on and around Muranowska Street.

The Hasidic shtibl as a place to gather arose as the movement itself gained steam in the late eighteenth and early nineteenth century. It originally referred to a room where Hasidim, usually a small minority of a town's Jews, would gather to pray in fellowship and following the somewhat distinctive, Kabbalistically-inflected liturgy of Reb Isaac Luria of Safed, known as the Ari. Various controversies arose as the central Jewish community organs of various towns saw these "breakaway" prayer gatherings as a threat to communal unity, authority, and fundraising, but attempts to have the government shut down these intimate and humble places of worship doubtless also strengthened the sense of solidarity among Hasidic men.[1] Such efforts seem in any case to have stopped by the twentieth century, much as Jewish reformers and modernizers continued to deride Hasidism. Moreover, as the movement became more popular and transportation easier (especially with the coming of railroads), small groups of followers of a particular Hasidic rebbe might be found in towns and cities far away from their leader's court. These small groups would strive to maintain their own separate shtiblekh—hence, not just "the Hasidic shtibl" but "the shtibl of the *x* Hasidim." The more popular the rebbe, the more such shtiblekh would be found throughout a given region of Eastern Europe; the larger the Jewish community, the more likely there would be a number of such shtiblekh there, each belonging to the followers of a different rebbe.

Nowhere were there more shtiblekh than in the metropolis of Warsaw—a city with some 350,000 Jews around 1910,[2] over half of whom were still Hasidim:[3] "Warsaw was home to no fewer than 442 shtiblekh where around thirty-five hundred native Warsavian youths studied alongside their Hasidic elders, bringing the number of full-time students in Warsaw alone to around five thousand."[4] While, as discussed below, the rebbes themselves had traditionally maintained their courts in smaller towns and many continued to do so, after the outbreak of World War I, "the capital soon became the home of fifty rebbes."[5]

Reb Zalmen centers on a very particular denizen of the Aleksander shtibl,[6] and also affords the reader an intimate look at the life of those who went inside to pray, eat, study, and argue there in the years between the two world wars. It is almost certainly fictionalized, but unlike some of Hofer's other writings about the narrator's family in Warsaw, it is not labeled a novel. It is hard to imagine that Reb Zalmen was not an actual figure, although finding any trace of him today would be a daunting task. This is especially so since Reb Zalmen was that rare thing, a traditional Jew without a known family. His last name is never given; in fact, all we are told, and all that his fellow characters in the book are given to know, is that he had originally come to Warsaw from the town of Shedlets, about 60 miles to the east. Although we never learn why he came, he was hardly alone in his migration. In fact, "The years before 1914 … saw a substantial increase in the Jewish population of Warsaw, which rose to 210,500 (33.7%) in 1897 and 337,000 (38.1%) in 1914."[7] The chapter on "The Handshake" (see below) even refers to a wave of speculative overbuilding in Warsaw, presumably in those years.

The exact timeframe of this book is difficult to specify from internal evidence. It seems safe to say, however, that most of it takes place in the decade or so following the end of World War I, possibly through the mid-1920s or so. The opening alludes to a photo taken during the German occupation of Warsaw during World War I and shown to the eponymous Reb Zalmen sometime later.

Moreover, that first chapter, titled "The Photograph," certainly is intended to suggest that Reb Zalmen was as real as the author/narrator's own family, ending as it does:

> "My father is no longer …
> "Reb Zalmen is no longer …
> "The photograph is no longer …
> "May their memories at least live on …"

Still, the precise degree of facticity in these stories is a secret that Hofer took with him. It seems likely to this reader that some rely more closely on his memories, while others involve more invention. Some historians today might find the latter worthy as well, perhaps as what historian Saidiya Hartman calls "critical fabulations."[8] Nearly all of them resonate with and provide either documentation or rich description of aspects of Polish Hasidism in the early twentieth century that are attested to by researchers in our day.

Regardless of Reb Zalmen's historical existence, that is, the book provides rich material for the historical ethnography of Polish Hasidism in the early twentieth century. Reb Zalmen himself comes across as something of the figure of an old Hasid from the so-called school of Przysucha (Pshiskhe in Yiddish). That school's "founder," if the term is not too strong for something that resisted institutionalization, was Yankev Yitskhok Rabinowicz, known as the Yid, or "Holy Jew." A former disciple of the "Seer" of Lublin, Rabinowicz broke with his own master and sought to establish something of a "reform" movement in Hasidism, focusing on introspection and scholarship rather than charisma and wonder.[9] Or at least, that is the image that has come down to us.[10] More broadly perhaps, the legacy of the Holy Jew and his successors continued decades later. "The case of twentieth-century Polish Hasidism suggests the ascendancy of a more sober, intellectualist model" than the more charismatic or popular-kabbalistic emphasis of earlier generations of Hasidic leadership.[11]

And indeed Aleksander, along with Ger and Vurke, was one of the largest Hasidic groups to stem from Przysucha.[12] The founder of Aleksander Hasidism was Shraga Feivel of Gritsa (Grójec in Polish), who settled in Aleksandrów Łódzki, near Łódź, following the death of his own teacher, Yitskhak of Vurke. The Vurker Rebbe was himself a disciple of the second Rebbe of Przysucha, Simcha Bunim; thus, Aleksander Hasidim, like most Hasidim in Central Poland, likewise had roots in what is known as the School of Pshiskhe. According to the YIVO Encyclopedia of Jews in Eastern Europe, the founder's grandson, Yeracḥmiel Yisroel Yitschak (1854–1910), was

> the most renowned member of this dynasty. He was a Talmudic scholar, and his reputation for wisdom made him an influential figure even among the non-Hasidic community in Łódź. He surrounded himself with a group of learned disciples; at the same time, he remained concerned about the spiritual needs of the ordinary Hasidim who were the majority among his followers. He was a strong opponent of

modernity, and his book, *Yismaḥ Yisra'el,* was considered one of the most important Hasidic statements about the dangers to traditional Jewish life and faith posed by modernization.[13]

At some or most of the time depicted in this book, the Aleksander Rebbe was Rabbi Shmuel Tsvi Dancyger, or—if and only if any of the action here is set after 1923—his son Yitzchok Menachem Mendel Dancyger, who was later interned in the Warsaw Ghetto and martyred at Treblinka.[14] Some of the Hasidic formations that stemmed from Przysucha were, as this suggests, genealogically dynastic—for example, the Rebbes of Biale (Biała) and Porisov (Parysów) were members of the same Rabinowicz family as the "Holy Jew." Others, like Aleksander and Ger, had originally followed an older pattern in which outstanding disciples, not necessarily descendants, became rebbes in turn. This may help to explain, for example, the concerns about possible "capture" of Aleksander Hasidim by the Rebbe of Biale that provides some of the drama for at least one chapter here.[15] More speculatively, the increasing turn to inherited leadership may help explain Reb Zalmen's reported disdain for almost any rebbe other, of course, than his own.

Hofer was a childhood friend of Abraham Joshua Heschel. Although young Heschel does not appear in this book, the figure of Reb Zalmen echoes several traits of Reb Menachem Mendl Morgenstern (himself a leading disciple of the Rebbes of Przysucha), the Kotsker Rebbe whom Heschel described in his masterwork *Kotsk: In gerangl far emesdikeyt* (Kotsk: The Struggle for Truth).[16] Like Reb Zalmen, the Kotsker—who is mentioned, albeit briefly, in this book—was always suspicious and dismissive of material concerns and motives, eager to strip self and others of egotistical pretensions, accordingly cautious that those called "Rabbi" not get swelled heads. Both the Kotsker and the fictional(?), historical(?) Reb Zalmen waited to pray each morning until they were good and ready. Both emphasized the primary value of Torah study.

Overall, *Reb Zalmen* describes a Jewish quarter of Warsaw where the Hasidim are still dominant, but their dominance is threatened. It gives the lie to older historiographic notions that Hasidism was on the wane by the early twentieth century and offers color and taste to supplement the recent research of scholars such as Glenn Dynner that argues for the continued vitality of this social formation. Indeed, Dynner describes Hasidism as a culture of resistance to internal colonization and assimilation.[17] Efforts to maintain the strictures of Jewish law such as those described in one of the first chapters here may be seen in that light—although the same chapter can also be seen as documenting the defections from Hasidic discipline caused, in part, by the shock and dislocation of the First World War.[18] The threat posed by any public transgression of those strictures was only enhanced by the fact that around this time, "residential restrictions had the effect of sifting prominent acculturated Jews out of historically Jewish neighborhoods while leaving behind a more heavily Hasidic mass."[19]

Although the book was published not much more than a decade after the end of World War II, it gives the impression of being remarkably faithful to the foibles, petty disputes, and everyday sufferings of Warsaw's Hasidim, rather than being retrospectively sentimentalized in the wake of the great catastrophe. That disaster nevertheless frames the book, in the opening vignette about "The Photograph" already quoted above, and in the coda that both documents Reb Zalmen's characteristically misogynistic attitude toward the narrator's expectations of earthly inheritance and suggests that the only true inheritance is memory.

Each chapter constitutes a story and is built around a certain episode, but much of each chapter is devoted to descriptions of the neighborhood, the shtibl, and its personalities. Each chapter, with almost no exceptions, then returns to its opening setup to crystallize and culminate in a moment of crisis. At the outset, the narrator/author explains that Reb Zalmen, the central character, was a regular guest at the narrator's family's table. Over the course of the book, his failures at various ventures are depicted, but he retains his own integrity, and his expectation of integrity from others, throughout.

Much of what makes this book compelling is indeed the way it weaves a humorous but ultimately sad portrait of the central character with descriptions of his larger lifeworld. Thus, for example, most of the chapter "Violating Shabbos" is not about Reb Zalmen himself. It presents the (at least until the moment when the story unfolds) fully traditional Muranowska Street, and a portrait of the Hasidim of another Hasidic rebbe, the deceased Rebbe Reb Moyshele Peltsevizner (who was in fact the father of Abraham Joshua Heschel). The chapter narrates the contrast between the initial ability of the Hasidim to maintain Sabbath order in the community and their eventual defeat at the hands of a Jewish storekeeper who insists on doing business on that holy day. The reader may wonder what it all has to do with Reb Zalmen until we return to the narrator's home. "Khilish" (young Yechiel Hofer) provokes Reb Zalmen, who as it turns out may not have even heard about this incident before. Reb Zalmen replies, unexpectedly but characteristically, that someone like that good-for-nothing storekeeper is not really capable of desecrating the Shabbos; *that*, God forbid, could only be accomplished by someone at the level of the Aleksander Rebbe or the Porisover Rebbe!

The next chapter, "Get Outta Here!" takes us inside the Aleksander shtibl itself. The third room in is the library. There are handwritten announcements in semiliterate Hebrew-Aramaic. As the various prayer quorums pass through, Reb Zalmen cadges cigarettes from them, smoking the best ones right away and saving the mediocre ones for later in the day. When he finally joins the last group of the morning, and declares the words, "Blessed is He who spoke and the world was," "he says it with such certainty and conviction as though he were standing before the whole world, testifying to what he had seen with his own eyes." The second part of the chapter depicts Reb Zalmen's zealous policing of the "no talking during Torah reading" rule. Reb Zalmen is so incensed by a violator of the rule that he comes out with the shockingly coarse Russian phrase, "*Poshol von*!"

Similar to some of Chaim Grade's memoiristic fiction depicting the Jewish quarter of Vilna around the same time, "Concerning the 'Threyter'" describes a scene that takes place when the narrator is already heading out of the traditionalist world described in the book. It begins with the explanation that by this time the author was no longer attending the Aleksander shtibl, but in the one called "Tarshish" (because, they said, that's where the ones running from God go). "And perhaps I wasn't praying at 'Tarshish' either by then. Could be, it's quite possible." This leads into a detailed narrative about an incident inside the Aleksander shtibl—an incident that, by his own explicit testimony, the narrator could not have witnessed. The narrator's pretend naivete ("please tell me Reb Zalmen, perhaps you can tell me what 'threyter' [Reb Zalmen's mispronunciation of "theater"] is?" is a perfect foil for Reb Zalmen's actual naivete. Yet curiously, this is the shortest, least developed, and least satisfying chapter in the book, almost as if the author were himself uneasy with it.

"The Rabbi Studies *Yoreh Deah*" pungently documents Reb Zalmen's suspicion of rabbis, and even of most Hasidic rebbes. The ditty that gives this chapter its title—describing a rabbi who appears to be absorbed in the minutiae of the law but actually cares only about the money he will earn from presiding over disputes, especially perhaps those between businessman—could be confused for a composition by the anti-religious Enlighteners, but somehow it seems rather to be the product of internal critique within the traditionalist Jewish world. Reb Zalmen's foil among the Aleksander Hasidim, Itshele Kubats, is described here in some detail. More generally, the reality of tensions and competition with the "traditional" world is elaborated. Reb Zalmen's opposition to the idea that Hasidim should try to obtain rabbinic posts is contrasted to the view of his own Rebbe: "The Rebbe held the opposite, that as many Hasidim as possible should become rabbis."[20] The story of Reb Zalmen's comeuppance in this regard is told as a Purim tale, affording the author a chance to describe exactly how funds were raised for charity from the congregation as part of the festivities. There is also a mouth-watering description of a Purim feast in a wealthy Hasidim home, including Lithuanian-style gefilte fish (with salt and pepper, rather than sugar) for the Litvak neighbors. Reb Zalmen's denial that the whole thing every happened is, perhaps, another intriguing twist of fiction.

In "Reb Zalmen a Businessman," some of the Hasidim in the shtibl try to come up with a scheme so that Reb Zalmen can earn at least enough money to pay for his own cigarettes, rather than having to cadge them all the time from others. The narrator's father proposes that Reb Zalmen set up a "store" to provide liquor and baked goods, to be sponsored and shared by those marking the anniversary of their loved ones' deaths. But Reb Zalmen is a reluctant and suspicious storekeeper who eats up the profits. Due to Itshele Kubats, Reb Zalmen's rule of immediate cash payment goes by the board, and his debtors fail to pay so that when he runs out, everyone has to take up a collection so he can get new stock. Eventually Reb Zalmen disposes of all his stock by giving a kiddush on the anniversary of someone's death—though he refuses to say whose, increasing the mystery of his origins.

When the narrator's father goes to the spa for a month, leaving the young narrator home with his mother and five sisters, Reb Zalmen is unwilling to sit and eat at the "women's table," and his refusal is the setup for "Reb Zalmen at a Strange Table." Reb Zalmen may not have been motivated solely by misogyny, since the narrator describes his sisters as speakers of Polish rather than Yiddish.[21] But he certainly avoids women whenever possible, and his denigration of them is contrasted to a sketch of the narrator's grandmother as a respected female Hasid of the Porisover Rebbe. The narrator's father arranges for Reb Zalmen to eat for that month at the home of Reb Shmuel, where Reb Zalmen doesn't find a warm welcome. We sense Reb Zalmen's awkward loneliness here and are also made aware once again that this book cannot be all memoir, given the narrator's absence from key scenes. Reb Zalmen's discomfort, and the poor and stingy meal he is offered here, come to seem like the narrator's revenge for Reb Zalmen's misogynistic abandonment of the narrator's family.

"The Handshake" may be said to explore some of the tensions in the particularly ascetic strand of Hasidism to which Reb Zalmen is devoted. Here he is seized by a sudden passion for money. Eventually he decides to become a marriage broker. He is rapidly made unwelcome and turns bitter. This leads to a back story: Once upon a time a man named Reb Avrom Borekh, neither a great Hasid nor a great scholar, was looking for a match for his only daughter. He was terribly afraid she'd wind up stuck with an ignoramus. Finally, he sends Reb Zalmen to test the scholarship of a potential son-in-law. Reb Zalmen goes to Aleksander for the High Holidays but forgets to go test the young man until the young man and his father are seated in a coach and about to set off for home. He must content himself with the young man's assurance that he "can learn," and a handshake on it. The groom turns out to be an ignoramus. When confronted, Reb Zalmen doesn't acknowledge his own fault but accuses the young man of falsely giving his word. Years later, when Reb Zalmen realizes that this old incident is the reason for his failure as a matchmaker now, he gives up on his dream and loses his passion for money.

Similar in theme perhaps to Y. L. Perets's famous story "Bontshe the Silent," where the protagonist cannot think of any greater heavenly reward than a hot roll with butter every morning, "Reb Zalmen's Worldly Pleasure" centers on Reb Zalmen's passion for a rich, fatty meat broth for lunch. This sketch describes various efforts to get Reb Zalmen regularly fed and taken care of. He is set up as a teacher of Talmud to young boys but is reluctant to instruct them. Arrangements are made to have a woman cook broth for his lunch every day, but he's dissatisfied that it's so thin and accuses her of stealing all the fat. When she gets sick, one of his students offers to cook the broth, and "fattens" it with castor oil, making Reb Zalmen dramatically sick. Reb Zalmen is cured of his passion for money, as is made clear in the next chapter ...

In "The Story of the Goose," Itshele Kubats insists that Reb Zalmen go to the suburban summer colony of Falenice to visit the gabbai Reb Shloyme who has become ill and lives there now. This entails a journey through and beyond the big, Gentile city beyond the Jewish quarter. Somehow by now we are so used to Reb Zalmen's "narrow" world that the realistic descriptions of the Gentiles on the tram (after they leave the Jewish neighborhood) seem at once alien and fascinating. We see these non-Jewish neighbors through Reb Zalmen's eyes, even though Hofer—who must have known the broader world of Warsaw well in his early adulthood—offers the reader realistic descriptions of everyday people going about their business. Meanwhile Itshele Kubatsh, who encounters hostile Polish Christians in his work every day, is satisfied that for once, Reb Zalmen sees what it's like for a traditional Jew to be among Gentiles. When they finally reach Falenice, Reb Zalmen is amazed to see a traditional Jewish summer-world. During the visit, the gabbai's wife offers him a goose, saying he can sell it back in Warsaw at a profit. But there's a Catch-22: anyone Reb Zalmen is willing to sell the goose to won't accept it (not knowing who slaughtered it, and thus unable to trust whether it is kosher), and the people who would accept it he won't deign to sell to. Finally, he sells it to a young man who is Jewish but clearly not religious, for a 20-zloty note that turns out to be counterfeit. From one standpoint Reb Zalmen gets his comeuppance for being so picky about whom he is willing to sell to; from another, his compunctions are confirmed as he is ultimately cheated.

If Reb Zalmen is thoroughly out of his element in non-Jewish Warsaw, there is a place away from the Jewish quarter where he is at home. That is the Rebbe's court in Aleksander, a town close to the industrial city of Łódź. Perhaps deliberately, Hofer sets "The Billy Goat's Yortsayt," the most folkloristic story in this volume, in a relatively non-urban setting—although in any case most Hasidic rebbes, even at this late period when so many of their followers were city folk, maintained their courts in such smaller towns.[22] The story features a goat who is somehow a reincarnated Hasid or at least "has in it a bit of a Hasidic soul." The goat is protected partly because it is a first-born, and partly because of its very Hasid-like (and Reb Zalmen-like!) behavior, such as staying close to the Rebbe's court in Aleksander and avoiding proximity to females. Reb Zalmen is especially partial to the goat. But the young Hasidim and eventually elders as well take advantage of the goat, riding it until one day it expires. The scene switches from the town of Aleksander to the Aleksander shtibl in Warsaw on a cold winter evening. The few Hasidim there want to make a little festive meal but can't think of an occasion, until the goat—or at any rate its memory—comes to the rescue.

In the next to last chapter, one Saturday evening in the shtibl Reb Zalmen calls the narrator over to study a bit of the Rabbinic collection known as Midrash Rabbah with him, as if he were trying to tell the narrator something very special and personal. Years later, on a day when Itshele Kubats happens to be at the narrator's home, the narrator wonders about the study session long ago and begins asking Itshele about Reb Zalmen. Itshele tells the narrator that everyone had assumed some personal catastrophe had driven Reb Zalmen from Shedlets to Warsaw. There is more that Itshele seems to know—but he stops before revealing it to the narrator, and hence we readers are kept in the dark as well.

If the primary setting of this book is the interior of the shtibl, there are several scenes that take place in the narrator's family home as well. Although, as already asserted, I tend to suppose that there was a living and not only imagined Reb Zalmen, one reason for skepticism is the way his perfect lack of family serves as a foil for both the narrator's rich family life and the loss of that family. In the end, Hofer writes, it seems that these "memories" are the only inheritance he has, and his hope is to share it … with us.

My immense gratitude to Ewa Bachminska, Barbara Kirshenblatt-Gimblett, and David Braun for assistance with the meaning of certain terms, and to Marcin Wodziński for precision regarding certain Hasidic groups.

Reb Zalmen

by

YECHIEL HOFER

Translated by
Jonathan Boyarin

CHAPTER ONE

The Photograph

We were sitting over lunch on Shabbos, after we'd finished eating the kugel and cholent. My father had just finished "Borekh Hashem Yom Yom," to the tune of a barcarolle that had somehow managed to make its way into the Aleksander *shtibl*. Nobody was in a rush to start eating the cold goose or the roast that had already been dished out. Our regular guest Reb Zalmen, whose memory wasn't what it had been in his youth, was repeating for perhaps the hundredth time Reb Mordkhe Yosef Izhbitser's commentary on the verse, "And the earth will not give forth its produce."

Just then my father stuck his hand into the breast pocket of his satin caftan, pulled something out and held it concealed in his palm, so no one could see what it was. Then he took the golden pince-nez hanging on a thin black silken ribbon tied to his vest button, and placed it on his smooth, narrow, chiseled nose. He spent some time looking at the object he held in his hand, and after he'd satisfied himself with looking, he placed it on the white tablecloth, in between me and Reb Zalmen.

It was a tiny, round, old, yellowed photograph. It showed a Jew with a gray beard, with sunken cheeks, a thick nose pointed at its end, a high, somewhat wrinkled brow, and a high satin yarmulke on his head. The person in the photograph was wearing an overcoat. His collar was surrounded by a rope, and a number was suspended from the rope.

My father explained that the photograph had evidently been cut out of a group shot, and that's why everyone wore a number. He supposed, he said, that the people in the photos had received passes from the Germans during the war. During the German occupation of Poland at the time of the First World War, they took group photographs of those who came for a pass.

I immediately recognized the person in the photograph and smiled to myself. Reb Zalmen looked at the tiny photograph for a long time and then shrugged his shoulders.

"Well, Zalmen," my father asked. "Who is that?"

Reb Zalmen picked up the photograph once again, placed it close to his eyes, then moved it away and stared at it from a distance, shrugged his shoulders again and said: "I don't know."

"Zalmen, look carefully," my father said. "Is it really possible that you can't tell who that is?"

Reb Zalmen stared at the photograph again. The he glanced at me as if he was trying to figure something out. Finally he gave up and put the photograph back down, saying: "I don't know."

"What do you mean, you don't know?" asked my father. "You can't tell who that is?"

"No, I don't know. It's not somebody I recognize," Reb Zalmen responded, slightly annoyed by now.

"Come on," my father kept insisting. "You really don't recognize him? That's Mordkhe Shedletser! How can you tell me you don't recognize him?"

Reb Zalmen quickly grabbed the photograph and excitedly said, "Right, right, that's Mordkhe Shedletser! Right! That's him indeed, that sinner! He slept on Purim right through the reading of the Megillah!"

Reb Mordkhe and Reb Zalmen were both from Shedlets, but almost no one remembered when Reb Zalmen had come from Shedlets to Warsaw. Anyone who knew the Aleksander shtibl knew Reb Zalmen. He was part of the shtibl, and that's where he kept a worn-out pillow and a threadbare remnant of a cotton blanket.

Reb Zalmen spoke with a Warsaw Yiddish accent, and if weren't for the fact that on occasion someone referred to him as Zalmen Shedletser, no one would have imagined that he wasn't a Warsaw native.

No one from Reb Zalmen's family ever came to visit him. In fact, no one even knew if he had any relatives, and nobody ever asked him.

As I've said, old age had weakened Reb Zalmen's memory. "Weak" isn't really the right word; there was something odd about it. He didn't remember much of what he had studied in his younger years, but he did remember things that no one else recalled. He distinctly recalled various Hasidic stories about bizarre events. In his world demons and spirits were entirely ordinary.

He was prickly. He had a sharp tongue, and he was extremely stubborn, always insisting he was right. He wasn't impressed by rich men, even though he himself was desperately poor.

He created big problems for us in the sukkah, where we sat alongside other Jews. He always started up with someone, and it didn't matter whether they were young or old, poor or wealthy. He picked arguments with Hasidim who weren't followers of the Aleksander Rebbe. At the drop of a hat he would shout, "Who are you? Must be a Kalibyaler faker."

Reb Zalmen loved to challenge convention. When it came to read the Torah portion Be'haaloskho (Numbers 8:1–12:16), he was outraged by the story about the quails: "And so what if the Jews in the desert wanted to eat a little meat? For that did they really deserve to be killed, to have a plague get to them?" he would shout, angrily banging on the table.

Reb Zalmen relied on his own judgment. Sometimes a dairy breakfast would be set out in the shtibl, and some doubt would come up about whether the cheese was kosher. Nobody else ate it except for Reb Zalmen, and he would boast later: "But me—I did eat the cheese!"

That thin little Jew with his little red beard like the flame of a *yortsayt* candle, Itshele Kubats, would tease Reb Zalmen, saying that he wasn't really strict about keeping Jewish law.

Reb Zalmen was very fond of money, though his own fortune certainly didn't amount to two Polish zloty. If someone gave him a valuable coin, such as a half zloty, he would smile with delight. The same Itshele Kubats said that Zalmen was so fond of money, if he owned a store he would certainly keep it open on Shabbos …

Reb Zalmen was short and broad, but with a bent back. The top half of his body preceded the rest. His beard was ash gray and his face was also ashen.

Reb Mordkhe Shedletser was quite different. He was tall, with good posture, sporting a short white beard. He was also stubborn and bitter, self-confident, but quiet and restrained. He spoke more with his eyes than with his mouth.

Reb Mordkhe had come from Shedlets about ten years earlier. He didn't live in the shtibl. Instead he had a bed somewhere, living with strangers to whom he paid rent each month. He had children in Warsaw, but they didn't pay much attention to their elderly father. They weren't interested in the commandment to honor one's parents. From time to time several of the Hasidim in the shtibl would get together and try to shame Reb Mordkhe's son, who was an ironmonger on Mila Street. But that didn't help much, and Mordkhe was deeply unhappy with the interference.

During the first years he spent in Warsaw Mordkhe was a glazier. Eventually he no longer had the strength to go from courtyard to courtyard with the pack of panes on his back, and survived somehow hand to mouth.

Reb Mordkhe and Reb Zalmen profoundly detested each other—the kind of enmity that only poverty can produce. They begrudged each other every spoonful of food they each received as charity. But Reb Mordkhe didn't openly express his contempt of Reb Zalmen. He never argued with him, but dismissed him with a wave of the hand as if to say that Reb Zalmen didn't exist. Nor was Reb Mordkhe ever heard saying anything bad about Reb Zalmen in public.

On the other hand, Reb Zalmen behaved submissively toward Reb Mordkhe and even flattered him. It was strange that Zalmen, who didn't cozy up to rich people, who had no respect for someone who happened to be sitting on the bench next to him, this same Zalmen who would pick a fight with anyone, who didn't even spare my father at whose table Zalmen sat and ate for many years, whom Zalmen often approached for a few pennies or for a shirt to wear the afternoon before Shabbos so he could go to the mikveh—in the presence of Reb Mordkhe that very same Zalmen would feel small and lost. So he would keep his distance from Reb Mordkhe, and in the latter's absence shamelessly insult him.

For a certain time both Reb Mordkhe and Reb Zalmen ate their Shabbos meals at our house. But it was clear that it was no good. Both of them were uncomfortable and cross. It became quite unpleasant. At every meal we were afraid that there would be a scandal. We decided that one of the guests would have to go. My father wanted to keep Reb Mordkhe and reject Reb Zalmen. But I wanted to keep Reb Zalmen. To me he was more interesting, more colorful, more lively. I liked his boldness, his "rebellions," and even the fact that he sometimes told my father off. I liked his bizarre stories. Apparently my father somehow liked Reb Zalmen too, and he did what I wanted.

Now Reb Zalmen sat at the table, holding the little photograph in his hand. He looked at it closely and spoke as if lost in thought. "Yes, that's him, Mordkhe Shedletser, that sinner, who slept through the whole reading of the Megillah …"

The photo wasn't of Reb Mordkhe Shedletser, but of Reb Zalmen himself. But Reb Zalmen didn't recognize his own face.

He didn't recognize the color of his own red-rimmed eyes, with which he spent so much time studying holy books. He didn't recognize the color of his ash-gray beard, which he would stroke from time to time. He didn't recognize the deep wrinkles on his parchment skin, which he would rub from time to time. He didn't recognize the earthen tones of his own face, nor the shape of his nose, which he used to blow so furiously. He didn't recognize the head that he carried on his tired, bent, wrinkled neck. He didn't recognize ...

Reb Zalmen never looked in a mirror, as he strictly observed all the implications of the ban on men dressing like women. Six days a week, with an unerring movement of his hand, he would place the tefillin on his close-shorn head. When he used to bow his head a bit in order to put those tefillin on, and slide his hand under his yarmulke to settle the straps along both sides of his skull, the tefillin would stay right where they belonged, in the middle, right above the fontanelle, the spot that had been waiting since before dawn for this moment.

So what use would Reb Zalmen have had for a mirror?

And why would Reb Zalmen have recognized his own face?

Where my father had come across Reb Zalmen's photograph I don't know.

My father is no longer—

Reb Zalmen is no longer—

The photograph is no longer—

At least their memory should remain ...

CHAPTER TWO

Violating Shabbos

On Warsaw's Muranowska Street, which Jews called "Board Mila," all of the stores were closed on Shabbos. Only the barber shop belonging to Starshi Feldsher, on the corner of Muranowska and Zamenhof, remained open. The Jews who lived on Zamenhof thought that the barber shop belonged to Muranowska Street, and the Jews on Muranowska were entirely convinced that it belonged to Zamenhof Street. In fact it belonged to neither street. The door of the barber shop, over which hung three brass platters, was set into a spot where the corner of the building had been cut at an angle. The corner was as flat as a nose pressed against a windowpane. The door within it had settled back into itself and couldn't be spotted from Muranowska or from Zamenhof. It seemed unconnected to any street, but rather to be a gateway into Gehennom ...

On Muranowska Street itself there were no pharmacies, no opticians, no barbers. Nothing interrupted the Shabbos rest.

The decorated shop windows, the doors with painted posters, the doors from which hung little display cases, all faced inside on Shabbos. From the street you could see their solid shoulders, covered with thick tin, secured by iron bars, on whose sides hung locks shaped like turtles, which kept concealed under their iron carapace the secret of their clever mechanism.

There were many Hasidic shtiblekh on Muranowska Street. A Sokhatshover shtibl, a Grozhisker, a Slonimer, a Lubavitcher, a Skernyevitser, a Porisover, a Peltsevizner known as the Rebbe Reb Moysheles shtibl, and others.

When Hasidim used to leave their shtiblekh with their velvet tallis bags under their arms, they covered the entire width of the sidewalk. The few non-Jewish residents of the street, the janitors, would remove their hats in greeting to their wealthy tenants. The Jews wore silk and satin. Their modest footsteps moved along the hard sidewalk softly, surely, and comfortably.

But one Shabbos the peace was interrupted. And on *Shabbos Hagadol*, right before Passover, no less.

Zelik was a bachelor. His father was long since dead. Zelik lived with his elderly mother and a sister, an old maid. He was short, with a pale face that was often moist with sweat. His front teeth were covered with gold crowns, and on the left side of his face an entire row of teeth were missing. He tried to conceal the missing teeth, and spoke only with the right side of his mouth, until eventually his mouth became habitually crooked. He wore spectacles attached to a golden chain that hung from his right ear.

He had inherited a small fashionable Jewish hat store from his father. Later, when Jewish hats went out of style, Zelik started carrying modern hats.

On Shabbos and holidays, Zelik prayed at the Rebbe Reb Moyshele's shtibl, which was right across the street from his store. The rebbe himself was already dead. But the shtibl stayed open, and Zelik enjoyed praying there, mingling with the Hasidim, chatting with them and having a drink at their *kiddush*.

Suddenly people noticed that workmen were busy at Zelik's store. Where a blank wall had been, the bricks were removed. The little store seemed to expand and now looked out open the street with two large show windows like two eyes wide open in surprise. On racks in the show windows hung all sorts of hats, black, brown, and green, for three, five or even twelve zloty.

Zelik had gotten married and received a dowry.

At night the show windows of Zelik's renovated store were covered with green-painted boards, then with iron bars, and secured with locks. The doors were also locked, but they could also be secured from within by two large chains.

At first the entire store, door and windows, was closed on Shabbos. Later, people noticed the superintendent of the building taking the boards away from the shop windows every Shabbos morning, and the hats would be on display all day. But the doors were still locked. Zelik kept coming to daven every Shabbos, and no one suspected what was happening inside the store …

Until one Shabbos, precisely Shabbos Hagadol, Moyshe Tallis-Maker, the *gabbai* of the Rebbe Reb Moyshe's shtibl, a sickly Jew who walked slowly along, noticed the door to Zelik's store open as he passed Zelik's on his way into the shtibl. Out of the store stepped a young man carrying a hat in a paper sack, which he tried to hide under his sleeve jacket. Reb Moyshe felt a stab strike his weak heart. He lost his breath. He stood stock still. Meanwhile the door opened again, and once again a young man slithered out, trying to conceal a paper bag containing a hat. Reb Moyshe immediately understood what was happening.

Meanwhile Reb Moyshe was joined by Reb Pinkhesl and Reb Khaskl, also Peltsevizner Hasidim. Others soon joined the three Jews. They started talking back and forth, and the discussion grew more heated. There were strong words, there were curses, fists were raised in the air.

Along came Henekh, a strong and solid Jew. He was a porter in the manufacturing workshops on Gensza Street. He also prayed at the Rebbe Reb Moyshe's shtibl. He was a simple Jew, but he had his place and his special role there. Every Yom Kippur eve he came to the shtibl with a rope that he wore around his waist all year. Jews threw themselves to the ground, struck their hearts in penitence, and Henekh counted out lashes with holy concentration.

When Henekh figured out what had happened, he was furious. He rushed toward the store. Meanwhile the door opened again and a head with two terrified eyes appeared in the doorway. Henekh set off toward the store and tore the door open with all his strength.

The crowd outside stood frightened and confused by what they were seeing. The store was full of young customers. Zelik stood on a ladder, handing down boxes of hats. His sister took the hats out of the boxes and gave them to young men to try on. At the cash register stood Zelik's bride, taking payment.

When Zelik saw what was happening in front of the store, he stood still on the latter for a moment with a stack of hat boxes in his hand. White as chalk, he didn't so much step as fall down from the latter, and this time without trying to conceal his missing teeth, he trembled as he shouted with all his strength: "Jews, go away, don't r uin me!"

"What? You sinner, trouble-maker!" came the shouts from all sides, and from all sides cramped, trembling hands reached out toward Zelik.

A moment later Zelik stood on the street surrounded by a crowd of screaming Jews, and behind him shut the doors of the store.

Reb Khaskl, a deliberate, thoughtful person, ordered: "Into the shtibl!" And before Zelik had time to look around, he was standing in the shtibl by the table.

"Sinner against the God of Israel!" thundered Reb Pinkhesl's basso.

"Let's carry out the sentence right here and now!" and Henekh raised his strong hands.

"Tear him like a fish!" the crowd shouted.

"Trouble-maker! Violating Shabbos in public on Muranowska? Have you ever heard of such a thing?" shouted Reb Pinkhesl at the top of his lungs.

Reb Moyshe Tallis-Maker, the weakling, appealed to Zelik's conscience: "Ay, Zelik, Zelik, who could have imagined that you would be the one to break ranks? And what will your father say in the Other World? Tell me, Zelik!"

"Let's carry out the sentence right here!" Henekh's hands reached close again.

"Tear him like a fish!" came the response once more from the crowd.

Zelik stood there pale, with beads of sweat dripping from his face. He could barely breathe, like a fish out of water. He opened his mouth and closed it again. It seemed as though he was speaking, but nothing could be heard. He made awkward, desperate gestures. He seemed to be asking for something, but no one knew what.

Reb Moshe Tallis-Maker the gabbai waved his hand and said, "Jews, let him speak."

Zelik took a deep breath, moved his lips a few times as if to see whether he could still move them, and from his mouth came quiet, confused words:

"Jews, it's hard to say, but without the money I earn on Shabbos I couldn't survive for one day. Throughout the week I don't earn a *groshn*. I only do any business on Shabbos. If I closed the store on Shabbos we'd have no choice but to die of hunger."

"*Shey-getsssss*—you're no Jew!" thundered Reb Pinkhesl, and the last consonant of the word long resounded between the walls of the shtibl.

"Do you hear what's going on here? He's trying to defend himself, that sinner. Instead of falling to his feet and showing repentance, pleading and weeping, banging his heart and asking us for forgiveness, he says that he has to keep the store open on Shabbos. You should die of hunger rather than violating Shabbos!" shouted Reb Pinkhesl, almost crazed with anger.

The congregation at the Rebbe Reb Moyshele's shtibl was poor. They were Jews who struggled to earn a living. They survived through hard labor. During the week they didn't have a spare moment to devote to Jewish matters. They cherished and caressed Shabbos like the last bit of jewelry of a man who was once rich. All week long they thought about Shabbos. Zelik's statement that he had to open his store on Shabbos fell like cold water on glowing steel, and in their anger and sorrow a painful shout emerged from their grimacing mouths:

"Tear him like a fish, no mercy, tear him up!"

Reb Moyshe the gabbai pressed his hand to his heart. He saw that the situation was serious, that it might lead to bloodshed. He called Reb Khaskl and Reb Pinkhesl to one side, quickly consulted with them, and told Yoyne the shammes to bang on the lectern to get everyone's attention.

"Yoyne and Henekh," he said calmly but loudly, "you go with Zelik. Let him get rid of the customers and immediately close the store. Do it in the wink of an eye. And you, sheygets," he said to the terrified Zelik, "must agree here before the assembled congregation that from today and henceforth *this* will never happen again." He emphasized the word "this," because he didn't even want to mention the words "violation of Shabbos."

Zelik, confused, shook his head to show that he agreed to everything Moyshe the gabbai had said. He muttered the promise that *this* would never happen again, and he quickly departed the shtibl together with Yoyne the shammes and Henekh the lashes man.

A few minutes later they saw the building super carrying out the boards to close the shop windows, and Zelik's store was locked and secured, inside and out.

But Zelik didn't keep his promise. As evening fell at the beginning of Passover, when the congregations had already gone into their shtiblekh to pray, Zelik's store stood open and customers entered and exited. The two show windows were brightly lit with electric bulbs. The colored hats were decorated with little flags, and each flag triumphantly proclaimed how cheap Zelik's hats were.

Jews stopped in front of the store. They called Zelik. But instead of Zelik, several fine young men stepped out of the store and told the Hasidim to go away, and quickly. They threatened to call the police. The crowd gave up and left in shame. A deep sorrow ruled in the shtiblekh and other prayer gatherings. People avoided talking about what had happened, like one avoids talking about an unpreventable disaster.

From that time on, Zelik's store remained open every Shabbos and holiday. On those days the store was so brightly lit that you couldn't look away, that it seemed as though the store was open on Shabbos and holidays and closed during the week. And perhaps that's what actually happened. The traditional Jews were as repulsed by the store as they were by crucifixes or monasteries. Jewish Muranowska Street lost its pride and self-confidence.

On the Shabbos Hagadol when Zelik opened his store, Zalmen, our regular guest, happened to be out of town. He was in Aleksander with the Rebbe, where he spent all of every Passover.

I waited impatiently for Reb Zalmen's return. I was so curious to know what Reb Zalmen, that passionate Jew, would say about the first public violation of Shabbos on Muranowska Street. I imagined what would have happened if he had been there that Shabbos.

And when Reb Zalmen did come back from being with the Rebbe I could barely wait to talk to him on Shabbos. Finally it came, and my father and Reb Zalmen returned to the house from the shtibl. I quickly greeted Reb Zalmen, and without even waiting to let him make kiddush, I spoke up: "What do you think of that story about Zelik, Reb Zalmen? I'm sure you've heard that he violated Shabbos in public, that he opened his store on Shabbos."

"Wha-a-a-a-t?" Reb Zalmen asked, and his red-rimmed eyes pressed closed so tightly that all one could see were two thin, red lines. Once again he said "Wha-a-a-a-t?" with a hissing, like the sound of an angry snake.

I was a bit uncomfortable with his "Wha-a-a-a-t?" My father looked at him with a puzzled expression. There was an odd stillness at the table.

"What did you say?" Ren Zalmen insisted. "Tell me, what did you say?"

I began to stammer again: "Well, probably you know, Reb Zalmen, that Zelik, the one who owns the hat store, Zelik violated Shabbos, he keeps his store open on Shabbos."

"Fool!" came the voice of Reb Zalmen like a lion's roar. I'd never heard a voice like that coming from him. "Utter fool!" he repeated, stamping his feet. "Who violated Shabbos? Zelik? You think that Zelik, that utter nothing, you think he can violate Shabbos? He can desecrate Shabbos? Stupid kid!" Reb Zalmen kept shouting, his beard and jaw trembling, his arms raised high in the air. "If you told me that the Aleksander Rebbe or the Porisover had violated Shabbos, well, I understand, that would be a violation of Shabbos, but that Zelik, that nothing, you think he can violate the Shabbos? You're dumb as a cow!" And Reb Zalmen gave me a look of contempt.

My father smiled. My younger sister and I, both of whom had doubtless tasted the forbidden pleasures of a violated Shabbos before Zelik, winked at each other. Somehow we sensed that it's not so easy to violate Shabbos, that it's not such a simple thing. We began to sense that perhaps we might never be able to violate Shabbos, that we might never get to that level ... Realizing this made me feel a little better, a little easier, a little freer.

Reb Zalmen reached for the bottle of liquor as if nothing had happened. As he poured the liquor into his cup he hummed a tune of the Vurke Hasidim. It was clear that Zelik's Shabbos violation hadn't impressed him in the least. That Shabbos his impassivity remained intact and proud. The slap of Zelik's open show windows fell short. And even though Muranowska Street might have lost self-confidence and felt that its Shabbos had been disturbed, in our house, at the table with Reb Zalmen, Shabbos reigned strong and secure.

CHAPTER THREE

Get Outta Here!

In the Aleksander shtibl on Zamenhof Street, which the Hasidim called "the big shtibl," there was one room, the third as you came in, that was devoted entirely to books. Around the walls stood simple, tall, wooden bookcases, painted with brown oil paint, with shelves of various sizes, on which books stood or were stacked. On the upper doors of the bookcases were posted announcements by rabbis lacking positions, or from Hasidim lacking income, addressed to the Aleksander Hasidim or to all Jews about various matters. Before Passover there were announcements posted by those who had hand-ground flour to sell for *shmura* matzo, kosher for those with the highest standards. Starting before the High Holy Days and until before Sukkes, one could see whole or partial sheets of paper concerning *esrogim* and *lulavim*. There was a Yiddish announcement from someone who had opened a barber shop where no beards were shorn and which was closed without fail on Shabbos. There were addresses where one could buy a Turkish tallis, a mezuzah, fringes, and other items related to Jewishness.

Most of the announcements were written in a strange Hebrew-Aramaic, often full of mistakes. Thus, for example, an announcement about shmura matzo ended with the words "And I bless our congregation and all of Israel with the kosherness of the holiday," instead of "with a kosher holiday."

The bookcases took up three walls of the room. And by the fourth wall stood a long, heavy, hardwood table. The table was constantly covered with volumes of the Talmud, of the *Shulchan Aruch*, or of *Eyn Yankev*. One always saw there the *Tana D'Vey Eliyahu* with its commentary *Ramosoyim Tsofim* and the book *Yismekh Yisroel* by the intermediate Aleksander Rebbe.

Along either side of the table there were two long benches, made of the same hard, heavy wood as the table. The benches were worn smooth and shiny from the years of sitting on them, as men rubbed against them with the rough material of their pants while swaying in study.

On the fourth wall, above the table, books stood on long shelves. All of the books, those in the closed bookcases and those on the shelves, were bound in coarse, gray-brown, homespun linen, and their names had been written on the spines with a chemical pen.

A group of youngsters, not the most talented of the students, devoted themselves to taking care of the books. They had a rubber stamp, an inkwell, and a receipt book. At various occasions such as a *siyum* or a *yortsayt* they would collect money for the upkeep of books. Thus they were able to rebind the books which had been used so long and so intensely that they had lost their spines and often their covers as well.

The same group of lads also undertook to get various people to donate books to the shtibl. Thus one could read on many of the flyleaves, carefully calligraphed: "This book belongs to the Hasid, the wealthy man and accomplished scholar Our Master Reb, and so forth." Sometimes the wealth and scholarship were nothing more than a fantasy dreamed up on the flyleaf. There were also various forms of declaring who the book belonged to. One of them was a particular favorite of the youngsters. He had written: "This book belongs. To whom does it belong? To the owner it belongs. Okay, to whom does it belong? It belongs to the one who bought it. Who bought this book? The one who bought it bought it. Okay, who bought it? The one who had money bought it. Who had money? The one who had it had it. Okay, who had it? Money had the grand and wealthy man, the remarkable scholar, the famous Hasid Our Master Reb So and So the Son of So and So."

Deep seriousness combined with high-minded joy reigned in the libraries of the Hasidic shtiblekh. Neither an Ark of the Torah nor a lectern for leading prayers was to be found there. It was a place dedicated not so much to devotion as to thinking, a place with less reality and more fantasy. Here a Hasid might loosen his belt and sometimes wear nothing but a yarmulke on his head. In summertime one could cool off in the shadows of the tall volumes of Talmud, indeed one could swim in its sea. In the winter one could warm himself with spicey analyses, with passionate conflicts of interpretation. A stove kept burning, two large electric lights illuminated the table and those studying around it, and youngsters poured tea from a large blue teapot. This was where festive meals and the *yortsayt* of various rebbes were celebrated, and here, too, the Hasidim ate more modest meals on any occasion. Quite often on Shabbos or on a holiday, a group of young men would gather there after praying early to make kiddush over a healthy shot of liquor and snack on something tasty.

Early every morning, summer and winter, Reb Zalmen would sit in that room with his back to the table. Next to him on the table, wrapped in a worn-out tallis-bag, lay his huge Turkish tallis with its heavy neckband and a pair of large tefillin. Reb Zalmen regarded small tefillin with the same suspicious hostility as a trimmed beard. As far as he was concerned, anyone wearing the supposedly more comfortable version, the light kind of tallis with tiny neckbands, wasn't taking his Judaism seriously. "Any Jew who wants his Jewishness to come easy is too easy on himself," said Reb Zalmen. Nor did he ever wear low shoes. In the heat of the summer he wore tall boots. "I'm like a soldier on the parade ground," answered Reb Zalmen when my father asked him:

"Zalmen, why do you wear boots in this heat? I'll give you a pair of my low shoes."

Reb Zalmen was a black study in the morning. His wrinkled brow faced downward. As always when he was dissatisfied, his red-rimmed eyes were almost closed. He chain-smoked. From time to time he lifted his head, opened his eyes, and looked through the doors into the room where Hasidim stood reciting their morning prayers. The minyanim succeeded each other so quickly that one began before the other had quite finished. Reb Zalmen sat there burning with anger at the "minyan factory." He couldn't stand to watch some of the Jews quickly removing their "leather-wear," as he mockingly called the tefillin of those who seemed to be in a rush. And he had no more patience for those who squeezed out slowly every letter of the service. He couldn't stand their bizarre gestures, their balled-up fists, their staring eyes. He couldn't stand the ones who showed off their piety by bending over triple at the phrase "We give thanks to You." He didn't believe they were really that submissive. He was consumed with suspicion. It seemed to him that everyone praying there had an ulterior motive. Some of them just wanted to give a false impression, and others were trying to fool God into giving them something. And he, Zalmen, who was terribly poor, sat there in attendance like a faithful watchman, trying to make sure that no one got something undeserved. He didn't even like the idea that they might deserve it. He only wanted to make sure that the prayer was performed "not in order to receive a reward," as it says in Ethics of the Fathers. As he sent two columns of aromatic smoke from his cigarettes through his nostrils, he felt like a partner of the Master of the World, assigned to make sure that there was no deceit. He wanted to make absolutely sure that nothing would come too easily for anyone praying at the shtibl.

From time to time Reb Zalmen would quickly get up from the bench where he'd been sitting since before daylight, and step into the room where everyone was praying. His short, bent body was almost lost among the tallesim of the congregation. Now you could see one side of his gray beard, then an arm wrapped in dark cloth, or a bit of his rounded shoulder. He made his way through the thicket of tallesim to borrow a cigarette from a young man who'd just come in. If he got a couple of good cigarettes, like "Egipskis" or "Mediums," he would take them back to the library to smoke. If he got a cheaper brand, such as "Grands," he'd hide them and continue looking to cadge cigarettes from the new arrivals.

Before daylight and early in the morning, when Reb Zalmen was angry and depressed, he only smoked good, strong cigarettes. He left the weaker and cheaper ones for later on, when he was in a better mood; by then it didn't make much of a difference to him what he smoked.

Reb Zalmen would sit for hours like this every morning. He couldn't bring himself to join a minyan. He had long since recited the first parts of the service, up through the first recitation of "Shema Yisroel," on his own. But he just couldn't be part of the congregation. It didn't feel right to him. He smoked cigarette after cigarette. The weekday commotion that blew in with the congregation was inimical to him. He shrunk into himself and couldn't find a place where he was comfortable. He didn't know what to do, and he got more and more upset. And even though the same thing happened every day, each time he felt the same shock and dismay.

It began to grow late. The congregation dispersed. The last few Jews, those who didn't have to run anywhere, arrived. Some of those who came late had nothing left of their efforts to earn a living except worry, and they weren't in a rush to worry. Often these latecomers would look around and realize they didn't have a minyan. They would go off to look for another two or three Jews, even those who had already prayed, just to be able to count them in the minyan. Then they would finally remember Reb Zalmen. They would go into the library, wait for him to finish smoking a cigarette, and bring him in to pray with them.

Reb Zalmen would unfold his broad, heavy Turkish tallis. Now an expression of calm composure spread across his face. Somehow it was easier for him, standing with this small crowd to pray. Since before dawn he'd been stubborn and downcast. He was afraid that what he was seeing and hearing wasn't as it should be. He was angry. Later he didn't even remember why he was angry, who he was angry at or what he wanted. Once he got into that strange mood he couldn't get out of it. But now when he stood wrapped in his tallis and recited the blessing "Who has commanded us to wrap in fringes," he suddenly felt better. All of his anger dissipated. His anxiety left him. His dark mood stopped oppressing him. He actually felt fortunate. And when he called out loud "Blessed is He who spoke and the world was," he said it with certainty, as if he stood before the entire world testifying that he had personally witnessed God speaking and creating the world.

On Shabbos and holidays Reb Zalmen prayed alongside my father, at the second minyan. That had been the pattern for years, ever since Reb Zalmen became our steady guest. On those days he was free of all his terrors and suspicions. In the morning he would go somewhere close by and drink a glass of tea, and then he'd return to the shtibl in time for the second minyan. When he arrived, he took off his heavy overcoat, put on his tallis and began to pray.

On those days the entire congregation of the "Big Shtibl" was divided into just two minyanim. When the first one finished, the second one prepared, and looked for someone to send up front to lead the service. When the second minyan was praying, a number of men who'd already prayed were still wandering around the shtibl or sitting and studying a holy book. There was no rush. Rich or poor, no one was busy calculating profit and loss that day. Nobody was trying to get anything that day. All they wanted was to be together as long as possible.

Reb Zalmen went along with the congregation's festive mood on those days. He sensed somehow that nobody needed his supervision then. He stopped wringing his hands. He was even ready to look aside and allow someone to get something he didn't think they deserved.

Still, he couldn't stop paying attention to the congregation altogether. There was something he remained concerned about, even on Shabbos and holidays.

Reb Zalmen was very strict about the ban on speaking during prayer, and especially during the Torah reading. To be sure, announcements hung, covered with glass, in every room of the shtibl declaring "It is forbidden to speak during the service and during the Torah reading." Nevertheless, every time there would be a crowd of younger married men and boys who'd gather in a corner and chat amongst themselves. When Reb Zalmen prayed it was harder for him to make sure no one was speaking. But during the Torah reading, he sat at the table, listening and watching to make sure that, God forbid, no one uttered a word. Itshele Kubats, the short Jew with a beard as red as the flame of a yortsayt candle, who always got involved with Reb Zalmen and loved to annoy him, said that Zalmen paid so much attention to make sure no one was speaking, so eager to catch someone in the act, that Zalmen couldn't actually hear a single word of the Torah reading himself.

When Reb Zalmen caught someone talking during the Torah reading, he would bang with both hands on the pages of the Bible that lay open before him. He made such a ruckus that the Torah reading would be interrupted.

Along with those who kept chatting, there was a group of fellows in the shtibl who were always asking questions. Over here someone was struggling with a long discussion in the book *Kli Yoker* and couldn't puzzle his way through it, and over there someone was having a hard time with a statement by the *Or HaChaim* that seemed self-contradictory if you weren't such a subtle reader—so they'd go ask someone else a question right in the middle of the Torah reading. Others simply had a question about a verse in the Torah portion. Most of these questions were addressed to Moyshe Efroyim Lipmans. He liked being asked, and he liked answering even better. He was good-natured and enthusiastic, especially about his own answers to others' questions. But to be fair, it must be said that he liked the fact that people were curious enough to ask. The desire to know, to understand, this kind of engagement with the Torah even on the part of those who understood very little, was precious to him. He would come to consult with anyone who had something to ask, and he paid no attention to the fact that meanwhile the Torah was being read.

Reb Zalmen utterly detested the questioners, and he equally detested Moyshe Efroyim Lipmans and his enthusiastic answers. In general he had no patience for religious enthusiasm. He considered the most extraordinary events to be entirely natural. Even the greatest miracle worked by a Hasidic rebbe, as long as it was his own Rebbe, required no further explanation. And lesser things? Nothing to get worked up about. He also didn't like it when people didn't know things. "What do you mean you don't know?" he would shout. "Are you sick or something?" And when it came to a real ignoramus, he would torment them, drive them away like demons.

More than anything, he resented someone deciding to ask a question during the Torah reading. It drove him crazy that he couldn't protest properly, since as soon as he began shouting and banging his hands on his Bible to make them be quiet, they would point to their own Bibles to show that they were just trying to understand what was written there. And what could he do then?

Obviously no one ever came to ask Reb Zalmen a question. They gave him a wide berth. He looked at the questioners with scorn, casting daggers at them with his eyes. If someone happened to pass by close to Reb Zalmen, carrying his Bible as he went to ask Moyshe Efroyim Lipmans, he would pass by like a smuggler trying to cross the border with precious contraband.

One Shabbos there was a question that troubled Borekh Dovid. Borekh Dovid was a rich man. He was no scholar, but he was a loyal Aleksander Hasid. He was thoughtful, quiet, well-mannered, and tall. He had a brown beard and wore gold-rimmed spectacles on his narrow, smooth nose. He wasn't one of the regular questioners, no! It just happened that today there was a verse in the Torah reading that puzzled him. He just had a sense there was something that he needed clarified. He raised his big eyes from the Bible he was holding in his elegant hands, and looked around for Moyshe Efroyim Lipmans. Then his glance fell upon Reb Zalmen, who happened to be sitting right next to him. Not thinking about what he was doing, not reckoning with the likely consequences, Borekh Dovid slowly stood up, and in all innocence approached Reb Zalmen.

Reb Zalmen noticed Borekh Dovid standing next to him. He understood that the latter wanted something, and muttered an irritated, "*Ni?*"

"Zalmen," Borekh Dovid began, "Zalmen, I wanted to ask you a question."

"Ha? Asking? And right when we're reading the Torah?" grumbled Reb Zalmen.

"Right, about the Torah," quietly answered Borekh Dovid.

"What kind of question do you have about the Torah?" asked Reb Zalmen, getting angrier.

Borekh Dovid barely managed to whisper, "There's something that's bothering me."

"Bothering you?" Reb Zalmen retorted with barely concealed fury. "And who said something that's bothering you?"

"I told you, it's in the Torah," Borekh Dovid stammered in confusion.

Reb Zalmen sprang upright. He was outraged. His shriveled face shrunk to half its size. His mouth twisted into a grimace, and through his remaining teeth came a hoarse, screechy voice: "Ha! The Torah's bothering you! You came to tell me the Torah bothers you? You have the nerve to say the Torah bothers you? *PASHOL VON*! GET OUTTA HERE!"

That Russian phrase, "pashol von," in a holy place, on Shabbos, during the Torah reading, coming from Reb Zalmen's mouth, was so shocking that it took everyone's breath away. For some time there was an unheard-of, perplexing silence in the shtibl. The Torah reader interrupted his chanting. Borekh Dovid retreated in shame. Then someone slapped his hand on a Bible. Cries were heard of "*Ni!*" and "*Mne!*" as everyone tried to express his outrage without speaking words. Soon everyone was banging their hands on their Bibles. The reader resumed chanting from the Torah scroll.

Reb Zalmen knew barely a word of any non-Jewish language. The few words he did possess came out of his mouth so mispronounced that it was hard to understand what he was saying. But that "Pashol von!" that he threw in Borekh Dovid's face came out in a pure Russian accent, as if his great-grandparents had all been Russians. All of his terrible anger, his deep hostility, his loss of self-control, his ecstatic zealotry—everything was poured into that "Pashol von!," the kind of expression that even a real Russian will rarely indulge in when he's angry. Reb Zalmen himself was frightened by his own anger, by his own use of those Gentile words. And when the reader began to chant the Torah portion again and the congregation had calmed down a bit, Reb Zalmen kept repeating to himself: "He wants to ask me about something that bothers him in the Torah ... the Torah bothers him ..."

After the service there was a dispute about the incident. Nearly all of the Hasidim held that Reb Zalmen had gone too far. "Bad words, rude words like that in a holy place! Really, insulting a Jew with such coarse words!" Some of those present held that "It's some nerve on the part of a penniless pauper like Zalmen to insult a rich man like Borekh Dovid." Reb Zalmen wasn't impressed. He wasn't troubled by those who thought he was in the wrong, and he was even less interested in those who took up his defense. He went to my father, who was standing among the circle of Hasidim, and called out: "Well, are you heading home now?"

For quite some time after this incident the group of questioners avoided Reb Zalmen. They knew better than to ask him any questions. Moyshe Efroyim Lipmans sat by himself on Shabbos, and no one went up to him. But Reb Zalmen still kept his eye on that gang. Indeed, he was even more watchful than before. Perhaps he sensed that after his outburst he wouldn't explode like that again. And perhaps he didn't want to be in that situation again, perhaps, who knows … Who can know? Who can say?

CHAPTER FOUR

Concerning the "Threyter"

By then I no longer prayed in my father's shtibl. I prayed in the shtibl the Hasidim called "Tarshish," that is—the shtibl for those who were running away from God, just like the prophet Jonah.

And perhaps by then I wasn't even praying at the "Tarshish." Maybe I wasn't praying at all. It's entirely possible.

But in any case, I always arrived home for Shabbos lunch ten or twenty minutes before my father and our guest Reb Zalmen returned from services.

As mentioned, Reb Zalmen was our regular guest. My sister Esther called him in Polish *żyd wieczy oyrekh*, "the Jew, the eternal guest," a play on words from *żyd wieczy tułacz*, "the Jew, the eternal wanderer."

One Shabbos I happened to come late. When I came into the dining room, my father and Reb Zalmen had already made kiddush, and the fish with its congealed sauce stood on the table.

I leaned over a bit and piously said three times, "Good Shabbos, good Shabbos, good Shabbos!"

My father replied with a dry and down-to-earth "Good Shabbos!" My mother said the same with slightly exaggerated warmth, evidently trying to smooth over the awkward moment. Reb Zalmen didn't reply at all.

But by that time my father didn't control my movements. He never asked me where I'd been or what I'd done.

I felt somewhat uncomfortable. I felt caught in a dilemma. Slowly and delicately I pulled back the upholstered chair, slowly sat down by the broad table covered with a snow-white tablecloth, modestly extended my hand, took the carafe of wine, poured myself a full glass and half to myself began reciting the preliminary words, "If you restrain, because of the Shabbos, your feet …"

When I finished making kiddush, I felt freer, more at home. I raised my eyes and looked around the room with more confidence.

I noticed that this time Reb Zalmen was in a better mood than usual, somehow more cheerful and self-satisfied. His velvet hat hung on the arm of his chair, his velvet yarmulke full of feathers from a poor, worn pillow stuck to his close-shaven head. Every few minutes he vigorously rubbed the back of his head with obvious pleasure.

Reb Zalmen was accustomed to making kiddush over a glass of pure alcohol. He didn't pour the liquor into his mouth like most drinkers do, but slowly slipped from it. When he'd finished sipping three-quarters of the liquid in the glass, he would put the glass down, take a pastry, recite the proper blessing, break the pastry, consider its insides, and slowly place a bit in his mouth.

Now he sat lost in an exalted mood, swaying back and forth, and singing between the kiddush and the fish course an old melody of the Rebbe of Vurke. He clapped his hands and shouted more than sang: "Oy vay, oy vay, oy vay, oy vay …"

I winked to my father and asked without words: "Ha? What's going on? What's wrong with him?"

My father smiled, and when Zalmen stopped singing for a moment, my father said: "Zalmen started a real rebellion in the shtibl today. He was quite the center of attention!"

"Really, Reb Zalmen? What was that about, Reb Zalmen?" I was dying to know.

Here's what had happened:

When the shammes at the shtibl, Hersh Khayem, gave the fourth *aliye* to Dovid, the son of the former gabbai Avrem

Borekh, a thin, blond young man got up from the bench next to the stove. He took his right hand and drew over his head the light tallis with its narrow neckband. (Today's generation is weaker than before, and who has the strength to wear a heavy Turkish tallis with a wide, silver neckband?) He gathered the two edges of the tallis close to his face so that his neatly trimmed beard wouldn't be quite so obvious, and approached quickly and directly (as one is supposed to do!) to the table where the Torah lay, covered with a dark blue velvet cloth.

He humbly bent over and reached out his hand to remove the cover. Suddenly Reb Zalmen appeared between Dovid and the table, shouting with his arms raised and his fists balled up: "You won't recite the blessing over the Torah. I won't permit it!"

"Zalmen, Zalmen! What's going on, Zalmen!" the shouts could be heard from all sides.

Zalmen waved his arms in front of him, stamped his feet, and shouted as loud as he could: "This sinner won't be allowed near the Torah!"

"Zalmen, what's with you, Zalmen? You're disgracing the Torah itself! Zalmen, why are you calling him a sinner?"

Zalmen's face was twisted in anger, turning red and gray at the same time. It was as if his gray face had merged with his ash-gray beard. He shouted angrily once again: "That sinner, that troublemaker won't make a blessing over the Torah, not while I'm alive!"

"Zalmen, what's going on here? Who made you the boss, Zalmen? Who asked you, Zalmen, whether he could be called up to the Torah or not?"

When he heard "Who made you the boss?" Zalmen stood up on the tips of his toes, squeezed tight his gray, red-rimmed eyes, and wagging his finger at the terrified young man, roared like a lion right in his face: "That sinner, that troublemaker goes into the 'threyter.'"

"Threyter, I say!"

In the uproar that followed Reb Zalmen's shout of that word "threyter," the young man Dovid Avrem Borekh disappeared.

"Yes," I said, "'threyter' is indeed a serious matter, but please, Reb Zalmen, perhaps you can explain to me exactly what 'threyter' is."

"He, he," said Reb Zalmen, wagging his finger in my face, "You don't know what 'threyter' is?"

My father hid his face. My mother didn't know what to do and made as much noise as she could with the dishes. My sister wiped her eyes with a little handkerchief.

"Zalmen," I said, "what nonsense are you saying? Do you really think I'm a 'threyter'-goer? I really want to know what the 'threyter' is."

My father could barely contain himself. My mother loudly ordered the serving girl to bring something. My sister covered her face and tried not to burst out laughing.

"Reb Zalmen," I said, "What do you think? Do you really believe I've forgotten who I am and where I come from? How could you possibly imagine, Reb Zalmen, that I know what 'threyter' is?"

Reb Zalmen glanced at my father. The sight of my father's lowered head interrupted Reb Zalmen's contentious and sardonic smile and his cackling laughter. And perhaps he felt sorry for my father. He bent over and began to whisper to my father in a serious tone:

I didn't find out what "threyter" is from Reb Zalmen. But he did tell me one thing: "As soon as you go into the 'threyter' you take off all your clothes ..."

And when Reb Zalmen had whispered the secret, a dark cloud appeared on his furrowed brow. He quickly covered his feet with the hem of his satin caftan, wiped his sweaty brow with his hand, rubbed his head with his yarmulke, placed his velvet hat on his head, and returned to the Vurke melody: "I will arrange my meal on Shabbos morning ... Oy-vay, oy-vay, oy-vay ..."

CHAPTER FIVE

The Rabbi Studies *Yoreh Deah*

1.

Reb Zalmen disliked rabbis. They were his enemies. He wasn't crazy about Hasidic rebbes, either. He would often say:

"Actually, none of those rebbes is even worth the time it takes me to speak ill of them. But if there is a rebbe somewhere that is worth it, then it's my own rebbe—and I mustn't say anything bad about him!"

Reb Zalmen reserved his greatest contempt for fat rebbes.

Once he went to pay a visit to an obese rebbe who had lived in Warsaw for years and had gotten sick. When Reb Zalmen came back the people in the shtibl asked:

"Well, Zalmen, what did you see there?"

"I saw a bed full of rebbe," Reb Zalmen angrily replied, and shook himself as if trying to get rid of a bad memory.

But that was nothing compared to Reb Zalmen's hostility to rabbis. He couldn't stand rabbis at all. He detested them individually and collectively. He couldn't listen to someone saying something nice about a rabbi. Instead, he seized on any insult, any bit of gossip like a precious jewel, like a rare find.

Reb Zalmen told a story:

"After the Baal Shem Tov died it was clear to everyone that his successor would be Reb Yankev Yosef, the author of the *Toldos Yankev Yosef*. But what happened? Something that astonished and distressed the whole world. After the Baal Shem Tov died, the holy *shkhine* took her satchel and handed it to the great Maggid of Mezritsh. Everyone who heard about it asked: 'Is it really possible? What happened here?' Those who understand these matters answered that it was because Reb Yankev Yosef was a town rabbi, the rabbi of Polonne. He dressed in a long coat with silken piping. And everyone knows that the Shkhine hates long coats with piping, and she hates rabbis …"

Reb Zalmen was a suspicious type. He suspected everyone and anyone. He suspected rabbis of all kinds of sins, but most of all he suspected them of taking bribes.

Reb Zalmen told a joke: "Once there was a rabbi who became deaf in his old age. They asked him, 'How could that be? We could understand if you'd gone blind, as the verse says: "Bribery blinds the eyes of the wise." But how is it that you went deaf instead?'

"And the rabbi answered: 'They always promised to bribe me, but they never paid up.'

"So now you understand," smiled Reb Zalmen, "that rabbi only sinned with his ears …"

Even though everyone understood this was just a joke, they also knew that Reb Zalmen took the matter of bribery very seriously. He didn't hold back his suspicions of any rabbi, even the ones well known to be saintly and honest. It didn't make any difference to Reb Zalmen. For him it was enough that the fellow was a rabbi.

Reb Zalmen's general assumption was that rabbis really didn't care about the Torah, Jewishness, the law, the decrees and judgments. They only cared about money.

When I was still a young boy and Reb Zalmen was still far from being an old man, he would call to me, take my hands, place them on the spot above my ears where my *peyes* would be, and teach me how to pretend I was twisting my peyes as I sang:

The rabbi studies Yoreh Deah
And he twists one *peye*
And all he thinks of is money,
Money, money, money!

Perhaps because I sang with the charm of a child, or maybe because my father enjoyed Reb Zalmen's satirical antics, my father often asked me to sing "The rabbi studies Yoreh Deah."

I came to enjoy the role. I began to add my own bits. I would sway back and forth in great concentration, twisting my imaginary peye slowly and with great concentration. I closed my eyes tight and slowly sang the words with great intensity. And my father was delighted.

Little Ithsele Kubats said that Reb Zalmen's enmity toward rabbis was simply a matter of jealousy. "Even just the idea that a rabbi could collect bribes, that's enough to drive Zalmen crazy. It drives him out of his mind. His jealousy of rabbis is absolutely boundless."

Itshele Kubats believed that Reb Zalmen loved money so much that if Zalmen himself had been a rabbi, he would have taken bribes at every opportunity. If two parties came to him for a judgment, he would have taken bribes from both sides. What's forbidden he would have permitted for money, and what's permitted he would have forbidden. He would have declared impure pure and pure impure. Anything for money. Kosher food he would have declared non-kosher and non-kosher kosher, just so he wound up making money. In the mind of little Itshele, Reb Zalmen turned into a monstrous, malicious force ready to destroy the whole edifice of Judaism for the sake of money ...

Reb Zalmen shouted that Itshele wasn't just brazen, he was also evil, ignorant, and stupid. He said that Itshele didn't know what he was talking about but had to state an opinion anyway.

But in fact, the little Jew with the red beard was quite learned in Torah. Nevertheless, when Reb Zalmen called him an ignoramus he didn't reply at all. In order to earn a meager living that had to support a family of nine, he couldn't spare even a couple of hours a day to study, and that depressed him and lowered his self-esteem. Itshele, who ran the whole shtibl and always had the final say, without whom nothing would have been accomplished in the shtibl, the same Itshele who was the Rebbe's "secret agent," before whom boys and young men trembled in the shtibl—he humbly accepted Reb Zalmen's declaration that he was an ignoramus.

Reb Zalmen himself claimed that he detested rabbis because they turned the Torah into a "spade to dig with," using it to make money.

Once when an Aleksander Hasid became a rabbi in a town, Reb Zalmen seethed: "What? He's a rabbi? He's just hungry! He needs bread, and he turns the Torah into bread. He needs bread, and his wife needs money for luxuries and that's how he winds up taking bribes."

The people in the shtibl tried to argue with him: "Zalmen, you must understand, Zalmen, that there have to be rabbis. Every congregation, every city, every shtibl has to have a rabbi, a local scholar to make rulings. So what would you prefer—that all the rabbis are Gerer Hasidim, and not one of them from Aleksander?"

"Look," replied Reb Zalmen with a smile, "I don't like the fact that the Gerer Rebbe has a single Hasid. But rabbis—as many as he wants. That I don't begrudge him at all. If he had a couple hundred rabbis, they would make sure he wasn't a rebbe anymore."

Reb Zalmen held that the reason why the younger folks were becoming spoiled, leaving Hasidism and Jewishness (the two being the same thing as far as he was concerned), was that Torah was no longer studied for its own sake, but turned into a practical tool.

"Torah itself is the most practical thing! Oy, Jews! What they've done with that useful thing! Oy, how they've subverted the real purpose!" shouted Reb Zalmen.

When an Aleksander Hasid who was a rabbi happened to be in Warsaw, Reb Zalmen would outright insult and torment him. And if the same rabbi was called up to the Torah on Shabbos with the title "The teacher our teacher," Reb Zalmen would stand right in front of the rabbi and mockingly stare him right in the eye. He would add out loud for the whole congregation to hear:

"Look at that 'Teacher our teacher,' a respected 'Teacher our teacher!' Look at what we've come to if that's a 'Teacher our teacher!'"

When an Aleksander Hasid became a town rabbi, everyone who formerly had addressed him with the familiar pronoun "*di*" began to address him formally as "*ir*," or else refer to him as the rabbi of the town where he had his position, such as "Tshekhanover Rov," "Aleksander Rov," etc.

But not Reb Zalmen. He didn't go along. It didn't matter that someone had become a town rabbi. Reb Zalmen continued to address him as "*di.*"

It didn't help matters when people reminded Reb Zalmen that as important an early rebbe as the *Oheyv Yisroel* had been the rabbi of Opatow, or that the *Kedushes Levi* had been the rabbi of Berditshev, or the Seraph, Reb Uri of Strelisk, had been a town rabbi as well.

"That was all long ago. It's not like that today. Today's rabbis are only interested in honor and money, honoraria for the clergy and flat-out bribes, and who knows what else too?"

"And what value is there in the way today's rabbis study?" Reb Zalmen continued complaining. "Does any one of them today look in the Talmud itself to find a reason for answering a question about Jewish law? And is there any such thing as an honest ruling by a rabbinical court today? It's just another business deal, just some more speculation, not a real deliberation in court. And what do you think they're studying, those rabbis? You think they studied the Talmud with *Tosafos* and the other commentators? Forget about it, they don't even remember who those guys are. And you think they learn the Shulchan Aruch instead? No, they learn the *Pri Megodim*, and sometimes just its abridged version." Reb Zalmen called the young rabbis the "*Pri Megodim*-abrigement-niks." That's what he called Moyshe Efroyim Lipman's son, who was studying to receive rabbinical ordination.

And Reb Zalmen became even more enraged when he heard about a rabbi who had sought to have his congregation agree that when he passed away, his son or son-in-law would take his position.

"What? Does he have a 99-year lease on the Torah? What? He decides who gets to inherit the Torah? He's holding onto the Torah so tight that he can leave it to his children?"

And if the son of a rebbe, who until recently had mingled with everyone, having a good time with all of the young Hasidim; when such a son of a rebbe suddenly began to be "dignified," behaving like his father did, keeping his distance, speaking slowly, walking modestly, sticking his belly out in front of him; when he started to separate himself from the Hasidic public, locking himself up in a separate room in the middle of the day, Reb Zalmen said: "See, he's crowing like a rebbe!"

But when that same rebbe's son started wearing a high fur hat like a rebbe, hanging around the rabbinic courtroom, interfering with matters of community concern, Reb Zalmen held that this was the height of arrogance and a swindle.

The Aleksander Rebbe found out from Itshele Kubats that Reb Zalmen insulted rabbis and said things about them that couldn't be tolerated. The Rebbe was very upset. The Rebbe had the complete opposite opinion. In the Rebbe's view, as many Hasidim as possible should become rabbis. He was absolutely convinced that only Hasidic rabbis, not *Misnagdim*, could save Judaism, and if the rabbis should be Hasidim, why shouldn't some of them be from Aleksander?

When Reb Zalmen came to see the Rebbe for the High Holidays, the Rebbe avoided letting him go at the end and wouldn't shake his hand. Reb Zalmen's thick nose with its sharp point grew white as a corpse. No one could tell if it had turned white from fear or from anger.

Although Reb Zalmen continued insisting that his hostility to rabbis stemmed from their turning the Torah into a practical tool, the fact that he spoke so often about bribery inclined everyone to agreeing with little Itshele Kubats that Reb Zalmen was actually jealous of the rabbis simply because they had the opportunity to take bribes ...

After the incident in which the Rebbe made Reb Zalmen stand for a long time, refusing to wish him "goodbye," the Hasidim began to think how to play a trick on Reb Zalmen that would make him stop once and for all gossiping about rabbis.

And Itshele Kubats was the head planner.

2.

By the time Purim approached, Itshele Kubats had the plan ready down to the last detail. Itshele had talked through the plan with several of the young men in the shtibl, and they were enthusiastic about it.

Just before Purim everyone in the shtibl, including the gabbai and the shammes, knew what was about to happen to Reb Zalmen. The only one who was still in the dark was Reb Zalmen himself.

On the evening of Purim, after the evening prayers and before the reading of the Megillah, when Reb Shloyme the gabbai and several of the most respected congregants of the shtibl were sitting at a table in front, when Hersh Khayem the shammes had already set before them the platters for *makhtsis-hashekel*, and Reb Shloyme had placed into one of the platters three old, silver Russian coins from the time of Nikolai I to represent the half-shekels ordained by the Torah, when one of the leading members of the shtibl, Reb Avrem Borekh who sat next to the gabbai, had taken out of his pocket and set on the table a long, white paper and pen on which to write exactly how much every member of the shtibl owed for *maos khitin*, Reb Zalmen began to approach the center of the table.

In previous years, when Reb Zalmen would approach the table and try to sit next to Reb Shloyme Gabbai and the other leaders of the congregation and start expressing his opinion about how much this one or that one should give, he had met with resistance.

This all happened during the first years of Reb Zalmen's residence at the "big" Aleksander shtibl in Warsaw. He was hardly an old man then, and he didn't command a great deal of respect. On the contrary, everyone considered it the height of presumption for Reb Zalmen, an outsider and an utter pauper, to push his way up front and decide how much everyone was obligated to contribute.

And every year Reb Zalmen didn't give up without a fight. He did everything he could to get to sit at the table. Sometimes he just managed to sit down there by force, but other times he was kept away and had to be satisfied to stand near the table or even a bit further off and deliver his biting comments to the stingy rich men.

But this time it was entirely different.

This time, when Reb Zalmen started approaching the table, not only did he not have to push his way through but the crowd parted to let him pass, saying "Let him through! Let him through!"

When Reb Zalmen reached the table itself, Reb Shloyme Gabbai and Reb Avrem Borekh, the sickly rich man, moved to make way for Reb Zalmen in between them.

For a moment Reb Zalmen sat there a bit perplexed by the unexpected honor he'd been shown. But just for a moment. His self-confidence was so strong that he quickly began to regard the honor as simply what he deserved. He only wondered why it had taken so long for him to be recognized in this fashion.

Reb Zalmen took the long sheet of paper lying before Reb Avrem Borekh and placed it where he was sitting. Thus he demonstrated to all and sundry that no one would contribute maos khitin money unless Reb Zalmen had first been consulted about the proper amount.

Reb Avrem Borekh didn't object when Reb Zalmen took the sheet of paper. He didn't act the least bit surprised. On the contrary, he took the pen and placed that, too, in front of Reb Zalmen.

Each year when the congregation came to the table to contribute for makhtsis-hashekel, Reb Shloyme the gabbai would take the three old silver coins out of one of the platters and place it in the donor's hand. The donor would then add whatever he could to the three coins, and place all of it in a second platter.

And that's how Reb Shloyme proceeded with each one. No one dared to take the coins out of the platter on his own. That was Reb Shloyme's responsibility year in, year out. He had the monopoly on it. He did it in leisurely fashion, without hurry, with due respect both for himself and for the donor.

Now, when Reb Zalmen sat down in between himself and Reb Avrem Borekh, Reb Shloyme Gabbai renounced his well-established role, and invited Reb Zalmen to be the one to hand over the three old silver coins to each donor.

But instead of the joy with which Reb Shloyme carried out this task, Reb Zalmen grumpily pulled the platter with the silver coins toward himself. Before he handed someone the coins, he would shoot them a surly look, as if thinking to himself: "Should I trust him with the coins or not?"

It wasn't the custom to argue about the amount of makhtsis-hashekel money demanded. Whatever the donor gave, he tossed into the platter. But Reb Zalmen kept a close eye as the donors gave, and no matter how much it was he muttered his dissatisfaction.

Reb Zalmen saw the congregation giving him funny looks. He was certain that they envied him the honor he'd been shown. That shored up his courage. He felt like a big shot, looking down at the congregants from above, and finally refused to look at them altogether.

Indeed, the congregation was giving him funny looks, but for an entirely different reason than the one he imagined.

On the night of Purim there were a number of people in the shtibl who had observed the Fast of Esther all day. They were eager to hear the reading of the Megillah, so that they could finally eat something. For their sake not a lot of time was spent in the evening on the contribution for makhtsis-hashekel or on maos khitin. That procedure was mostly left until the morning.

Early on Purim morning Reb Zalmen sat at the head of the table. He no longer considered makhtsis-hashekel money worthy of his attention. He was only interested in dealing with maos khitin. He held the pen and paper, and whenever anyone arrived Reb Zalmen didn't bother to ask him how much he intended to give. Instead he took the paper and wrote a sum of money there.

The sums that Reb Zalmen inscribed on the sheet were far beyond the capacity of the donors. One by one the people stood before Reb Zalmen, humbly asking him not to be so demanding and reduce the sums he'd decided on.

But Reb Zalmen was spreading his wings and enjoying his power. He didn't want to hear a word from anyone. He sensed that his day had finally arrived, and it seemed to him that he was flying over the heads of the crowd with the white sheet of paper and the pen in his hand …

People shouted at him: "Zalmen, you're robbing us blind! You don't have a Jewish heart, you have a Tatar's heart! How can you be so cruel, especially when it comes to charity?"

"Zalmen, how can you be asking me for so much maos khitin, when I don't even have enough for myself for Passover? What do you think you're going to get from me with extortion?" shouted an anguished Jew, who could barely scrape two pennies together.

But Reb Zalmen was sure of himself. He didn't want to hear their sob stories. "If you really want to give, you'll have it," he declared.

Reb Shloyme Gabbai and the other respected Jews who were sitting nearby at the table smiled into their broad, carefully combed beards. Reb Zalmen thought that they were smiling because they were satisfied with his strict demands, and the expectation that there would be plenty of maos khitin this year.

But they were smiling for an entirely different reason …

As mentioned, this all happened in one of the first years of Reb Zalmen's residence at the Aleksander shtibl in Wsrsaw. It was also the first year he was our regular guest.

My father waited for Reb Zalmen so they could go home together to the holiday lunch. But Reb Zalmen was so wrapped up with the money business that he didn't even notice my father. Finally my father went up to Reb Zalmen and said: "Zalmen, I'm going home. When you're done, come right away. We'll wait for you."

We started on the fish without him. But we did wait for him before serving the chicken soup with *kreplekh*. Reb Zalmen eventually arrived looking cheerful, quite pleased with himself. He clapped his hands like a bird that flaps its wings before it takes off.

Reb Zalmen had already had more than one drink at the shtibl, and he was somewhat tipsy. But mostly he was in a good mood because of the honor he'd been shown, and everything he'd personally accomplished that Purim.

Reb Zalmen washed his hands and recited a blessing, took another drink and another, ate the fish and egg challah with appetite, then the kreplekh and the rich broth, the meat and the special Purim *tsimes*. He smoked a strong cigarette, drawing deeply then exhaling two columns of thin smoke through his nostrils. Just like Purim should be. And he didn't neglect to stay something nasty about a rabbi.

"That new *moyreroe* (rabbi) Ruven wanted to get out of giving maos khitin. I said to him: 'Listen you, you think that just because you became a *khaye ro'oh* (wild beast) it means you aren't obligated to give charity anymore?' And I wrote down a sum for him to give—he'll cry, but he'll give it. I won't have to abide by his ruling; he'll have to abide by mine," boasted Reb Zalmen.

Reb Zalmen began singing the song "Shoshanas Yankev" to a tune of the Vurke Hasidim, the only one he knew, but the tune that fit well with the words of some of the Shabbos hymns didn't fit "Shoshanas Yankev." It came out somehow as a sort of cheerful moan. My father began teaching Reb Zalmen a lively tune that fit well with the words, but Reb Zalmen didn't have a head for melodies and my father let him be.

The telephone rang, and my father had to go into the store. We recited grace after meals. Reb Zalmen went off to have further discussions with Reb Shloyme Gabbai about maos khitin.

3.

Before the first stars were visible at night we sat down to our real Purim feast.

Electric lights hung over the white tablecloth, and on the table sat a candelabra and candlesticks. The table was covered with dishes of various types and flavors: sweet, sour, salty, and peppery. There was a chocolate torte so dark brown it was almost black, surrounded by a coulis of white cream and covered with candied apples, pears, and plums. The honey cake was covered with a thick, shiny, golden-brown crust. It gave off a scent of baked almonds along with honey, cloves, and orange peel. A glass bowl contained almond cookies cut in half, and squares of shtrudel. In a polished glass dish lay homentashn, shiny brown, filled with poppy seeds, and others made from yellowish shortcrust dough filled with chopped red beets and soaked in honey. That was my grandmother Brayndl's specialty, and it was my favorite. In addition there was a *teyglekh* confection and *farfel*, also soaked in honey.

The honeyed pastries, the tall beakers filled with golden Hungarian wine, the strong old mead and the silverware made the entire brightly-lit table shimmer gold and silver, shining with plenty and luxury.

For those guests who would only drop in or for those who came to collect alms, there was set out on the side marinated herrings whose delicate silver-blue skin looked appealing. From the kitchen came platter after platter of *chrusciki*, light as paper, dusted with powdered sugar.

On the table there were platters of fish, stuffed and unstuffed, cooked with sugar in the Warsaw style or with salt and pepper in the Lithuanian style. The Lithuanian-style fish was made especially for our neighbors in the courtyard on Pokorna Street, for the lawyer and for Breitman, both of whom were Litvaks. There was also marinated fish.

There were various meat pies and the main dish of the Purim feast, a whole side of roasted young veal, lying on a large plate, surrounded by various vegetables.

My father sat at the head table in his satin caftan and velvet cap. Right in front of him he set piles of silver coins: guldens, twenty-kopik pieces, half and whole rubles. In addition he had placed paper money in the breast pocket of his satin caftan.

Frequently the bell would ring and in would come a gaggle of singing Hasidim. They danced through the hallway and into the dining room singing "Shoshanas Yankev." They stopped dancing, sat down, had a bit to eat, made fun of the torte, expressed their opinion of the shtrudel, and set off again.

Folks from the shtibl arrived two by two, with worried faces, hardly looking Purim-festive. They sat down next to my father, slowly ate the refreshments, and spoke quite seriously to my father. Then my father would hand them something out of the piles of coins, or pull out of his pocket a bill, each one according to his merit and needs.

On a table near the wall stood the *shlakhmones* that had been sent to us. Tortes, long boxes filled with dates, wine, mead, cognac. Most of the bottles of cognac were covered with a sort of glittering straw, and the bottles bore a blue label depicting two barefoot Jews in long clothes bearing a huge bunch of grapes on a pole. The boxes of dates depicted a setting sun, a camel caravan, and a few date trees.

I wasn't especially interested in the food, not even in the shlakhmones or the guests. I was waiting for the Purim players we were expecting. But my father disliked Purim players. He didn't allow them to come in but just arranged for them to be given a coin and told to be on their way. They only managed to sing the first lines of a song:

"I'll gladly hand over my last bit of kasha
"Just let me study a page of Rashi."

And then in Russian

"*ti razboynik molodets*
"*ya razboynik molodets.*"
(You're a fine bandit
I'm a fine bandit.)

With that my father would push some money into their hands and beg to be excused.

This year I was especially eager to see the Purim players. I'd heard that our neighbor Brody's younger son, along with Shmukler's and Bavarnik's boys, had gotten together and rehearsed the story of the sale of Joseph.

I waited and waited, and then they arrived. The bell rang, and in raced a tall youngster in a long shirt bound with a belt, with a red helmet on his head and a long stick in his hand. He banged on the floor and sang out in an artificial basso:

"Clear out, clear out
"On all four sides.
"Here comes Uncle Yankl
"With his twelve fellows."

But I didn't get to see Uncle Yankl and his twelve fellows. My father muted the tall lad with a big coin, and they didn't play for us. My Purim was ruined. I was angry at my father. I heard, though, that our neighbor Brody was also offended, because my father had been rude to his son, refusing to let him into the apartment.

From early evening on, Reb Zalmen sat with us utterly contented. He didn't eat much, but he did drink wine and mead and kept smoking the strong Smyrna cigarettes in their brown papers.

His ash-gray face grew red and shiny. The wine and mead had their effect. He took off his hat and sat in his feathered velvet yarmulke. He sprawled on the upholstered chair, feeling like each and every limb of his body was a creature unto itself.

It was as though Reb Zalmen's brain was surrounded by a dense cloud, made up of the brandy, wine, and mead he'd been drinking all day, and various thoughts mingled in that cloud, thoughts of the wonderful days to come. He sensed that there had been a big change in the shtibl, and it was all to his good. He felt like the saintly Mordecai, covered with glory at the end of the story. The minutes and hours passed slowly, like the wine he sipped from his glass. Reb Zalmen forgot that he'd have to go back to the shtibl and lie down on a hard bench. He felt like this Purim was stuffed to the brim with miracles, and it would always stay that way.

My father kept refilling Reb Zalmen's glass, and Reb Zalmen didn't even notice. It seemed to him that the glass never emptied, that every sip was his first. He completely lost any capacity to reckon time or number. The ground began to waver under his feet, the world began to waver, to fly by …

At first Reb Zalmen frowned seeing my father distributing the piles of money. But the more Reb Zalmen drank, the more generous he felt. He even began smiling as my father distributed alms, as if to say that he, Reb Zalmen, approved of the deal. Nevertheless, when my father reached his hand into his breast pocket and took a large bill—somehow that still tugged at Reb Zalmen's heart.

Hasidim started to arrive. Some of them didn't want wine, but only beer. Along with the beer came chickpeas. Some of them were soft and some hard with wrinkled skin like old men, and they were thickly sprinkled with pepper. Everyone partied with Reb Zalmen, made toasts with him, wished him a happy holiday, and praised his accomplishments regarding maos khitin.

There weren't that many Hasidim at our home. Everyone there had been invited and was someone we knew well. Among them was Itshele Kubats. He was extraordinarily cheerful, even though he hadn't drunk much. He sang "Shoshanas Yankev" to various tunes. Then he danced in his stocking feet on the tips of his toes.

Just then two young men from the shtibl burst in, shouting excitedly: "Zalmen! Where are you? The whole shtibl is waiting for you. Everybody's been there for a long time already, but you're just sitting here! They paid for us to bring you back in a coach, Zalmen, where's your coat? Come, the coach is waiting!"

Even though Reb Zalmen's head wasn't clear enough for him to carefully consider what was going on, he somehow sensed that it wasn't how it looked. He couldn't remember a Purim when people had gotten together to drink in the shtibl. On Purim people either stayed with their family or went to the home of a wealthy Hasid where a small group of friends might gather. On top of that Reb Zalmen didn't feel like leaving us, and anyway he could barely stand on his own two feet.

But when he heard "Zalmen, the whole shtibl is waiting for you" and he saw that they had come to pick him up in a coach, he couldn't sit still. The honor he'd received Purim evening and just now led him astray. He reckoned that if the whole shtibl was waiting for him, perhaps he'd better go there indeed.

And then the young men started in again with "Zalmen, what are you hanging around here for? Zalmen, everybody's waiting for you!" and Itshele Kubats shouted, "Come, Zalmen! I'm coming too. Dovid! Shloyme! Aren! Come on, let's all go to the shtibl."

They helped him into his coat. They practically carried him down the stairs. They got him into the coach and set off for the shtibl.

4.

When Reb Zalmen entered the shtibl, all of the electric lights were on and candles were lit all over as well. It was bright as Simchas Torah.

Absent from the shtibl were Reb Shloyme Gabbai, Reb Avrem Borekh, and all of the respected fellows who had sat at the table with Reb Zalmen during the makhtsis-hashekel donations. Only the young men were there. Reb Zalmen was very pleased. He enjoyed the company of young men and boys.

The young men accompanying Reb Zalmen shouted: "Step aside for Reb Zalmen! Step aside!"

Everybody moved back to let Reb Zalmen through, and he was directed to the center of the table by his entourage, led by Itshele Kubats.

They opened a new barrel of beer and handed the first glass to Reb Zalmen. After the wine and mead, which had made him so lightheaded that he felt like he weighed nothing and could hardly feel his own body, that single glass of beer made him suddenly feel as heavy as if he'd ingested bars of lead. He sat there paralyzed.

They handed Reb Zalmen another glass of beer, into which the little Jew Itshele Kubats had poured a bit of brandy. Reb Zalmen already had the mixed taste of brandy, wine, cognac, and mead in his mouth, and hardly sensed that it wasn't a regular glass of beer.

They kept handing him glasses of beer, and Reb Zalmen felt like his brain was on fire. But suddenly the fire went out. His head was filled with a heavy black cloud, and his mouth itched with thirst. His narrow, red-rimmed eyes were like thin little cracks. His ears felt as though they were stuffed with cotton, and everyone's voices came like echoes from far away.

Reb Zalmen desperately wanted to drink something, but no one would offer him anything more except water.

Meanwhile the youngsters kept singing "Shoshanas Yankev" and dancing.

All at once one of the young men shouted: "A rabbi! A rabbi!" and everyone else shouted along: "A rabbi! A Purim rabbi! We must have a Purim rabbi!"

Reb Zalmen hardly perceived the word "rabbi." All he could hear was a wild murmur: "Wooo! Wooo!" It sounded like the howling wind, and he sensed a sudden cold striking deep into his bones.

"Zalmen! Reb Zalmen, Rabbi! Reb Zalmen will be the Rabbi! Reb Zalmen, Reb Zalmen!" the crowd shouted in mad enthusiasm.

Soon the little Jew Itshele Kubats and several other young men were standing next to Reb Zalmen. They stood him up, brought over a rabbinic-style high fur hat and a long satin coat, and before you knew it Reb Zalmen was wearing the sacred vestments.

They sat him back down at the table. Reb Zalmen plopped down as if he'd just shed a heavy burden. His reddened eyelids flitted this way and that as if he was trying to catch what was going on.

Seeing Reb Zalmen decked out in rabbinic finery, the crowd howled.

Itshele Kubats banged on the table and shouted: "Shut up, you bums!" And from every corner someone picked up the words: "Shut up! Be quiet! Sha!"

Itshele Kubats called out in his high-pitched voice: "Reb Zalmen the Purim Rabbi will honor us with a sermon!"

"A sermon! A sermon!" everyone repeated.

Itshele Kubats bent down and shouted in Reb Zalmen's deafened ears: "A sermon!"

Reb Zalmen moved his lips like a fish out of water. Somehow he managed to stammer a word here and there: "the earlier authorities, the later authorities, responsa, Reb Yoynesn Eibeschütz's *Urim v'Tumim* and his *Kreysi uPleysi*," but his words didn't contain a coherent thought. Nobody understand what he was trying to say.

Itshele Kubats shouted: "Enough! Enough! Mazel-tov! Mazel-tov!" and the crowd repeated: "Mazel-tov, Rabbi! Mazel-tov, Purim Rabbi! Mazel-tov!"

With all the noise and confusion Reb Zalmen felt utterly lost. But at that moment fragments of memory began to sneak into his muddied brain. He began to remember that he had been shown great honor. Like someone desperately ill who suddenly senses that good and faithful hands are taking care of him, Reb Zalmen looked at the crowd standing around him, and he smiled.

From a corner of the shtibl appeared a costumed character with a stiff red beard, wearing a smock underneath which peeked a black, greasy undershirt. Next to him walked another man with a huge black beard, also wearing a smock and an undershirt. In front of them walked a thin little Jew with a pointed beard and a frightened face, holding by the esophagus a brownish-bluish lung of a cow.

They approached Reb Zalmen and the thin little Jew sadly asked, "Reb Zalmen, we'd like to know whether this lung is kosher."

Itshele Kubats took the lung from the little Jew's hand, passed it to Reb Zalmen and ordered: "Blow!"

Reb Zalmen, utterly lost, began blowing into the lung. But he barely had any breath. He panted and he gasped, but he couldn't inflate the lung. The Jew with the red beard gave Reb Zalmen an angry look. He grasped both sides of his smock and pleaded, "Rebbi! If you declare the cow unkosher, my wife and children and I will have to go begging! Rebbi, have mercy!"

Reb Zalmen removed the esophagus from his mouth and looked at the man. The man came right up to Reb Zalmen and pressed into his hand a hard silver coin.

Then the man with the huge black beard stepped up and bellowed in a hoarse voice: "Rebbe! I'm a partner in that cow. If you declare the cow unkosher, there's nothing left for me to do but kill myself!" And he, too, came closer to Reb Zalmen and pressed a coin into his hand.

Itshele Kubats grabbed the lung from Reb Zalmen's hands and shouted: "Kosher! Kosher!" Everyone echoed the ruling: "Kosher! Kosher!" They took up once again the melody of "Shoshanas Yankev" and started dancing.

Meanwhile a young man appeared dressed up as a woman. He had tied a kerchief around his jaw as if suffering from toothache and managed to cover up his beard. He'd used his belt to arrange the tails of his silken caftan so cleverly that it looked like he was wearing petticoats. His head was bound in a large handkerchief whose ends covered the top of his overcoat. This "woman" and her "husband" approached Reb Zalmen concerning a divorce.

Little Itshele Kubats began interviewing the "woman" about intimate matters between husband and wife, and the tipsy crowd doubled over in laughter. Meanwhile the "woman" approached Reb Zalmen and pressed a coin into his hand. Itshele Kubats shouted: "The woman should be a bit further away!" Then the man approached and also gave Zalmen a coin. Itshele called out: "Come tomorrow to hear the ruling!"

More people came to ask the Purim-rabbi for rulings about kashrut or to hear their dispute, and every one of them pressed a coin into his hand. Reb Zalmen took the money without thinking, not knowing what was going on but still eager. He placed every coin into the breast pocket of his silk overcoat.

When Reb Zalmen's pocket was full of money, little Itshele Kubats ordered: "Everybody sing!"

Reb Zalmen thought he heard the crowd singing:

Reb Zalmen studies Yoreh Deah
And he twists one *peye*
And all he thinks of is money,
Money, money, money!

When this was finished, Itshele Kubats got up on the table and began talking: "Zalmen, Zalmen! Listen, Zalmen! You deserve a good slap, and actually a real lashing. Purim is like Yom Hakipurim. On Purim you can ask for forgiveness for all of your sins and transgressions, just like on Yom Kippur. So really it would be proper, Zalmen, for us to give you forty-two good lashes, and you should strike yourself for belittling the honor of rabbis and thereby belittling the honor of the Torah.

"But if we don't give you a beating, it's because you need to know, Zalmen, that you need to have respect, you have to make sure not to insult not only a real rabbi, but a Purim-rabbi as well.

"And you, Zalmen, insulted this very day our new rabbi, Reb Ruven! Instead of calling him *moyreroe*, 'Rabbi,' you called him *khayo roe*, 'wild beast.' I'm telling you now, Zalmen, that on Shabbos you must approach him in your stocking feet and accept his reprimand. If you don't do that, we'll really pass judgment, and you'll be barred from the shtibl.

"And I'm also telling you, Zalmen, that a Jew can't be cruel, even when it comes to collecting alms. The entire list of payments that you drew up for everyone to donate is useless, because you were cruel." With that, Itshele pulled out the long list with its large sums that Reb Zalmen had so proudly assembled, and tore it up in front of Reb Zalmen: "On account of you, Reb Shloyme Gabbai and that invalid, Avrem Borekh, have to go up to every member of the shtibl one by one and put together the proper moyes-khitin list, this time without being cruel.

"And now listen up good, Zalmen. You've said all kinds of nasty things about rabbis. The main thing you accused them of is taking bribes, even though I'm sure you've never seen it happen. But we really did see you shamelessly taking bribes in front of everyone who's here. You declared an obviously non-kosher animal kosher, you said impure was pure, you even took a bribe straight from the hand of a woman!

"So I beg your pardon, Zalmen, but please give back the bribes you took. At least you won't be carrying around those idols in your silken caftan!"

Even though Zalmen was so loaded with alcohol that he certainly couldn't tell the difference between "Bless Mordecai" and "Curse Haman," when he heard that he had to give the money back, he suddenly sobered up. He shouted at Itshele Kubats in wild fury: "Robber! Murderer!"

"Ha, you see?" cried Itshele. "The Talmud says that a man is known by three things: by his cups, his pocket, and his anger. Today we know you by all three, Zalmen! Now we know why you kept insulting rabbis. You just envied them the chance to collect bribes! Grab him!" Itshele ordered again. Several young men seized Reb Zalmen, took out all the money in his pockets including the few little coins he really owned, and disappeared.

Reb Zalmen collapsed onto the bench where he'd been sitting and fell into a long, solid sleep. Hersh Khayem the shammes related later that when he'd arrived in the shtibl late the next morning, Reb Zalmen was still out, and he could barely wake him up.

Later, when they tried to tell Reb Zalmen what had happened to him that Purim, he denied the whole thing. He had never been drunk, he had never been a Purim rabbi, he had never taken a bribe. It was all in the mind of that nervy little bastard Itshele Kubats, who picked on Reb Zalmen mercilessly.

Of course, Reb Zalmen was still Reb Zalmen, and no one really demanded that he accept a reprimand from Ruven the rabbi. Of course, no one ever really dreamed of banning Reb Zalmen from the shtibl. On the contrary, there were some people who held that Itshele Kubats had gone a bit too far, been too brazen in his attack on Reb Zalmen, even if it was Purim. All the same, given that it was indeed Purim and everyone was drunk, they forgave Itshele for the prank.

But two things were accomplished that Purim:

Reb Zalmen continued to insult every Hasidic rebbe except his own. He insulted *misnagdim*, Hasidim, the rich and the poor, pretty much everyone who came to mind, but he never insulted rabbis again. To be sure, nobody knew what he thought of them privately. But in public—never.

And one more thing: the next day, Shushan Purim, Reb Zalmen remembered that on Purim itself he had forgotten to recite the evening prayers. He sat down at our family's table in the afternoon and started drinking, and then they brought him into the shtibl, and he forgot about praying.

From that point on Reb Zalmen took upon himself to announce in the shtibl every year on Purim, that as soon as there were three stars in the sky, before everybody had too much to eat and drink, they would recite the evening prayers. Reb Zalmen kept up that custom all his days.

After he died, when people sat down at the table on Purim, whether at the home of a relative or a Hasid they knew, someone at the table would say: "Reb Zalmen." With that, everyone would stand up to recite the evening prayers.

CHAPTER SIX

Reb Zalmen a Businessman

1.

Reb Zalmen was practically addicted to cigarettes. He always had one in his mouth, and sometimes he would light the next one from the one he was finishing. The part of his thick white mustache over the middle of his mouth was yellow. It looked like a bit of steel wool stuck to his nose.

Reb Zalmen was an expert inhaler. He would place the smoke somewhere deep inside, hold it there, and meanwhile keep up a conversation or study out loud. But suddenly people noticed that words were coming out of his mouth wrapped in similarly sized, round, grey-white clouds of smoke. His breath smelled of smoke, and when he spoke to someone up close one could smell a mix of different tobaccos.

Of course, Reb Zalmen didn't buy his own cigarettes. He was desperately poor, and cigarettes weren't cheap. Reb Zalmen simply took the cigarettes from others.

Whenever somebody came in and Reb Zalmen knew he was a smoker, Reb Zalmen would go right up to him and demand a cigarette. He would do this all day long. Occasionally he would cadge several cigarettes from the same person on the same evening.

Itshele Kubats said that Reb Zalmen couldn't resist his lust for a smoke. And if a Jew gives in to one kind of lust, he'll give in to other kinds as well. Little Itshele imagined that Reb Zalmen was full of all kinds of lust ...

Reb Zalmen was well aware of the things Itshele said about him, and he just smiled. He really didn't care. It was odd to see how Zalmen, who became furious when someone threw the least hint that he wasn't a sufficiently devoted Hasid, didn't pay any attention to Itshele's suspicions about Reb Zalmen's indulgence. On the contrary, somehow it seemed that Reb Zalmen actually enjoyed the suspicions.

No one refused to give Reb Zalmen a cigarette or two. But people in the shtibl began saying that Reb Zalmen was debasing himself by constantly bumming cigarettes.

That didn't trouble Reb Zalmen. He didn't feel humiliated by taking from others. Sometimes it bothered him that they didn't offer the cigarettes without his asking, but he didn't think twice about asking. Except when he felt insulted; then he would burst out with a fiery retort.

A few of the Hasidim in the shtibl sat down to consider what to do about the situation. They wanted to figure out how Reb Zalmen could at least earn enough money to buy his own cigarettes, or at least some of them.

Reb Zalmen was offered the job of writing out requests on behalf of women who went to see a certain rebbe. But Reb Zalmen wouldn't hear of it. "Lord preserve us, dealing with women all day!" he shuddered at the very thought. Nor did he want to become the assistant of the shammes Reb Hersh Khayem, who had been serving in the post for decades. Reb Zalmen didn't plan to become a shammes, let alone an assistant.

So my father, who believed in the value of the merchant class, came up with the idea of turning Reb Zalmen into a businessman.

Every day a few of the people in the shtibl had yortsayt. To mark the anniversary, they would offer everyone in the shtibl a shot of liquor after the morning prayers in honor of the soul of the deceased. Each time someone had to be sent out to buy liquor and cookies. My father said that Reb Zalmen should set up a little "tavern" in the shtibl, where he could keep liquor and snacks. He could charge a bit more than the price in a real tavern, and with the difference he could afford to buy his own cigarettes from time to time.

Reb Zalmen liked the plan. He was willing to deal with liquor and snacks. He was really enthusiastic about the idea, and rubbed his hands in anticipation of his new business.

No sooner said than done. My father provided Reb Zalmen with two jars of herring, one schmaltz and the other marinated. Enough money was collected for Reb Zalmen to buy several quarter-liter bottles of alcohol, thirty water *pletslekh*, and ten egg cookies. Hersh Khayem cleared a shelf on one of the bookcases where worn-out volumes used to lie and put all the contents of the "tavern" there. And Reb Zalmen became a storekeeper.

2.

Reb Zalmen took his business very seriously. He was very proud of his wares. In the morning there were several minyanim in the shtibl, and Reb Zalmen knew very well that someone was observing a yortsayt at almost every minyan. But he didn't approach them to ask if they needed something from his store. Rather he sat in the back room with the books, and waited for people to come ask him to do them a favor and sell something. If someone came and said to him, "Well, Zalmen—give us a bite to eat," he would give the crowd an angry look, slowly stand up, calmly walk to the bookcase, slowly open it, take out and put into his breast pocket a bottle of liquor, carry the jars under his arms and the pletslekh and egg cookies in his hands, and only then enter the big room where the crowd was waiting.

Reb Zalmen set everything on the table and the one who was observing the yortsayt would offer more or less to the crowd, depending on what he could afford.

As mentioned, Reb Zalmen was very suspicious. He didn't trust anyone. Now, when he placed his wares on the table and arranged it all, he kept a close eye on everything going on around him. He counted each glass of liquor consumed, the pieces of herring and the pletslekh. Little Itshele Kubats, who loved to torment Reb Zalmen, always tried to trip up Reb Zalmen's accounting. Now he took two pieces of herring at once, now he drained an extra shot of liquor and denied it, just to give Reb Zalmen a hard time. He made Reb Zalmen so angry that Reb Zalmen would grab the bottle of liquor off the table, pick up the snacks, close his tavern and refuse to sell anything else, even when people were ready to pay in advance. Only after long entreaties was he willing to open his tavern back up and provide refreshment.

Reb Zalmen insisted on cash payments. When the drinking and eating were finished, he would count up the total and the person observing yortsayt had to pay right away. Not only was he unwilling to lend on credit, he didn't even want to accept collateral. Only "cash on the barrel," he insisted.

Just at the time when Reb Zalmen opened his tavern in the shtibl, the Aleksander Rebbe came to Warsaw. The Rebbe was well acquainted with Zalmen, and knew he was a pauper. He had never asked Zalmen what he lived on, nor had Reb Zalmen ever complained about money or asked the Rebbe to help him earn a living. The notion of livelihood was beyond the scope of Reb Zalmen's thoughts and desires. But apparently this time the Rebbe had been told about Reb Zalmen's new business. And when Reb Zalmen greeted the Rebbe, the latter asked him: "Well, Zalmen, how are things going for you?"

The Rebbe's question didn't make much of an impression on Reb Zalmen, and he answered: "I'm doing fine. I set up a little tavern in the shtibl. If I make money—that's good. And if not—I eat it up myself."

It was all the Rebbe could do to keep himself from laughing out loud. He bent his neck from side to side as he sat on his chair. The brim of his wide plush hat first met his right shoulder, and then his left. "Well," said the Rebbe, "it's the first time in years that a Jew hasn't come to me complaining about earning a living. On the contrary, he tells me that thank God he's doing well."

After the Rebbe said that, Reb Zalmen's tavern became famous. People started coming from other Aleksander shtiblekh to have a drink. Reb Zalmen poured himself into his work. Several older Hasidim began to mutter that the congregation was more interested in Reb Zalmen's tavern than in study. People started snacking not only after the morning services but in the evening as well. The younger men had a good time. The boys who usually weren't allowed to take any liquor gradually began to mix in with the older crowd. Some of them didn't have any money and had to borrow from their friends. Eventually they wound up in debt. Reb Zalmen's tavern was the big news in the shtibl, and business was going just fine ...

Until one day a wealthy young man who on some occasion had ordered Reb Zalmen to set out generous amounts of liquor and snacks for the crowd let Itshele convince him to go along with a practical joke.

After the crowd had drunk and eaten at the rich man's expense, Reb Zalmen waited to be paid in cash. The young man turned to him:

"Zalmen, I don't have any money on me. I'll pay you this afternoon. I forgot my wallet at home this morning."

Reb Zalmen flushed with anger. Then he started on a rampage. He pushed aside and threw to the floor anything he could reach. He cursed the young man with fire and brimstone.

The crowd in the shtibl took the side of the young man. They shouted at Reb Zalmen: "Zalmen, what's with you? Who do you think you're talking to? Why are you afraid to give him a loan? You should only wish that he owed you as much as he could afford to pay you back!"

But Reb Zalmen paid no attention to them.

The young man quickly regretted the whole business. He was angry at Itshele for convincing him to tell Reb Zalmen he didn't have any money and thereby causing such a ruckus. He was thinking of telling Reb Zalmen that he was only kidding, taking out his wallet and paying Reb Zalmen what he owed. But his rich man's pride was touched, and he responded to Reb Zalmen in a cold, low voice: "Well, Zalmen, in that case you'll have to wait until the day after tomorrow."

"As far as I'm concerned you can pay after Messiah comes," Reb Zalmen said, as if abandoning all hope of payment.

The young man didn't wait until the day after tomorrow to pay, and he didn't even wait until the afternoon. Half an hour after he left the shtibl, he returned and paid Reb Zalmen what he owed. But it wasn't much comfort to Reb Zalmen. He took the money, but he didn't take the same pleasure in it that he usually did. He didn't even count the money. He felt that he had been violated, that something deeply wrong had happened.

3.

And Reb Zalmen's premonition was correct.

From the day the young man refused to pay up right away, nearly every time someone ordered drinks and refreshments, he somehow wasn't able to pay the full bill right away. It always turned out that the person observing a yortsayt didn't have enough money to cover what had been consumed.

At first it was no big deal. Twenty *groshn* might be short, or half a *gildn* or even a whole one. But as time went by the shortages became more and more common. Eventually it reached a point where a Hasid, by no means wealthy, said to Reb Zalmen after ordering drinks and snacks for the crowd: "Zalmen, I don't have any money today. I'll pay you as soon as I can."

Reb Zalmen had no choice but to start keeping accounts. At first he remembered all the amounts owed in his head. But when little Itshele Kubats decided to give him a hard time and claimed in public that Reb Zalmen was demanding repayment of the same debt twice over, Reb Zalmen began writing down the debts on a piece of paper.

But even that wasn't enough for little Itshele. He convinced a group of youngsters to pick the sheet of paper with the amounts owed from the bottom pocket of Reb Zalmen's caftan.

The kids had a great time following Itshele's orders. They liked Itshele's sense of fun and the pranks he used to play. They didn't like Reb Zalmen because he was always angry and shooed them away.

When Reb Zalmen noticed that his account sheet had been stolen, he saw red. He shouted that he was ruined, that he'd been cheated, that the tavern was failing. "Drunkard! Glutton! Bankrupter!" he yelled at Itshele Kubats who seemed to organize everything going on around Reb Zalmen.

Now that people were more and more frequently buying on credit from Reb Zalmen, he rarely had any money when the liquor or snacks ran out and he had to buy fresh supplies. Instead, before every purchase people had to raise money to support the tavern. No one mentioned or even remembered that Reb Zalmen was originally supposed to earn enough profit so that he could occasionally buy his own cigarettes.

In truth, the consensus was that there wasn't really any more point keeping the tavern in the shtibl. But just like Zalmen himself, his tavern had become a fixture in the shtibl and it was hard for people to give it up.

During the week Reb Zalmen always prayed with the last minyan. Most of the people who came to that minyan were elderly and poor, and they weren't very busy. Usually there were barely more than ten, and more than once some of them had already prayed.

Naturally, in such a small minyan the occasions for yortsayt were few and far between. And when someone did have yortsayt, he didn't usually offer everyone a drink.

As long as Reb Zalmen was able to demand immediate cash payment for the liquor and snacks, it didn't bother him that the poor last minyan didn't drink, even when someone had yortsayt. It was obvious that if you didn't have money, you didn't drink. But when the earlier, larger minyanim began making partial payments or taking everything on credit, it began to bother Reb Zalmen that the poor minyan didn't drink.

Reb Zalmen advised the members of the last minyan to gather amongst themselves a few groshn every morning, so that when someone did have a yortsayt, there would be money to pay for a drink. They listened to Reb Zalmen and collected some money, but when a yortsayt came around there still wasn't enough for liquor and snacks.

Reb Zalmen himself offered to lend the difference. Bit by bit, the poor minyan became indebted to him. They paid the debt out of the money they had raised, but it wasn't enough. One time a member of the minyan had yortsayt, and there wasn't a penny in the liquor fund. So Reb Zalmen allowed him to take everything on credit.

With that, Reb Zalmen finally lost any interest in business. He regarded his tavern as a ruin, a remnant, a shard, neither fish nor fowl, neither dead nor alive, and somehow the whole affair had been spoiled for him.

Reb Zalmen was a zealot. He wanted everything to go one way or the other, hated compromise, hated ambiguity.

Reb Zalmen stopped counting the shots of liquor consumed, stopped counting the cookies or pletslekh they ate. He started taking everyone's word for how much they owed. Over time he stopped keeping a record of the debts. Eventually he stopped demanding payment as well. If he was paid—good; if not—that was good, too. It was all the same to him.

When people realized that things had changed with Reb Zalmen, that he wasn't the same as he used to be, they started paying their debts both sooner and completely. No one waited for Reb Zalmen to count up how much had been consumed. Rather, one of the drinkers would take responsibility for seeing how much they'd had, the crowd itself would figure up the total and hand Reb Zalmen the correct amount. People started borrowing less and paying cash in full more often.

Nevertheless, Reb Zalmen had lost his enthusiasm. The whole thing felt alien to him, as if somehow the tavern had given up the ghost. Now, even more than before, he would give the poor minyan drinks for free.

No one understood what had happened to Reb Zalmen, and the most curious among them was Itshele Kubats. He couldn't understand why Reb Zalmen had suddenly lost interest in business and money. He thought that Reb Zalmen loved money so much that he once jokingly insisted that if Reb Zalmen owned a real store, he would keep it open on Shabbos. He couldn't figure out what had changed. He started a rumor that Reb Zalmen wasn't in his right mind.

4.

One Friday evening before minchah the crowd at the shtibl learned that Reb Zalmen had yortsayt and was getting ready to lead the evening prayers.

Until that moment no one had ever heard of Reb Zalmen observing a yortsayt. Presumably he did, but he had never said anything to anyone about it. He'd never even asked to be given an *aliyah*. Presumably on those occasions he would have said kaddish discreetly to himself, somewhere off in a corner. But this time he did announce that he had yortsayt and demanded the right to lead the prayers.

Right before *kaboles shabes* Reb Zalmen approached the table on which lay the tallis that Hersh Khayem had laid out for the prayer leader, picked it up, quickly unfolded it and tossed it over his shoulders. Before anyone could utter a word, Reb Zalmen stood at the lectern and in a hoarse voice cried out the opening words.

Reb Zalmen couldn't sing. He only knew one melody of the Vurke Hasidim, and it came out more as a shout accompanied by clapping than as a song. Now, when he reached *Lekha Dodi* he wanted to use that very same tune. But the crowd began to sing an upbeat march tune instead. They sang so loudly that the words of the hymn were entirely drowned out as they struggled to emerge in Reb Zalmen's confusion.

On Shabbos morning Reb Zalmen got up to lead the morning prayers. Everyone assumed that he would stop at a certain point and leave the rest to someone who really knew how to sing and lead the congregation, as was the custom in the shtibl. But when Reb Zalmen reached the paragraph *Shoykhen Ad* and everyone began to bang on the tables to signal that Reb Zalmen needed to stop and let someone else take over, he acted like he didn't even notice them. Instead he grasped his right ear with his right hand and a cry tore out from his throat: "*Shoykhen Ad*!"

What could the crowd do? On the other hand, when Reb Zalmen wanted to just talk his way through the beautiful hymn *El Adon*, the congregation took up a barcarolle which had somehow made its way into the Aleksander shtibl. Reb Zalmen stood there perplexed, unable to fit the words to the melody.

When it came time for the Torah reading Reb Zalmen insisted that Reb Shloyme the gabbai give him *maftir*. But this was an honor that was sold at the shtibl on Simkhes Toyre for the whole year to come. If someone who had yortsayt really wanted maftir, he had to arrange it with the person who had bought it then. Reb Zalmen intervened until they finally gave it to him.

After that, naturally Reb Zalmen led the *musef* prayer as well. And as soon as he finished the last words of the mourner's kaddish, he hurried up to the table, banged on it and announced loudly that everyone was invited to his kiddush and no one should leave beforehand.

That really amazed everyone. The fact that he'd led the prayers—indeed, his very mentioning that he had yortsayt—that was already remarkable. But Reb Zalmen inviting everyone to a kiddush, that was almost incomprehensible. And precisely for that reason even the rich men who never stayed when someone in the shtibl offered a kiddush stayed behind, if only out of curiosity.

Reb Zalmen grabbed his tallis, took it off and put it down on a bench without bothering to fold it. He went into the library, the same room where kiddush was always made. He removed all of the books from the table, straightened out the tablecloth that had been placed on it before Shabbos, and set the benches around it—all with the competence and efficiency of a young man. Then he removed from the bookcase everything in his "tavern," leaving nothing behind.

Then he went back to the room where everyone was slowly removing their taleysim and putting them away in their bags. "Come on, everybody! Kiddush is waiting!" Reb Zalmen called out cheerfully. People began to arrange themselves on the benches. On the table stood five bottles of liquor. There were egg cookies and crackers, along with plain and marinated herring. There was plenty for everybody. Reb Zalmen was totally absorbed in the mitsvah of hospitality. He made sure everyone had a place to sit and had a drink and something to snack on.

It wasn't the same Reb Zalmen but someone consumed with passionate concern for his fellow Jews. He even brought his nemesis, little Itshele Kubats, a glass of liquor and waited to listen while Itshele made kiddush.

As for Reb Zalmen himself, he stood up while making kiddush and having a bite to eat. He cried out happily, "And he stood before them," like our Father Abraham did before the angels. It wasn't the same Reb Zalmen as the one who could sit and drink glass after glass without showing the effects at all. This time he became quite tipsy. Still he went from one to the next, urging them to eat and drink.

But after all there wasn't so much to eat and drink, and the crowd made quick work of what was offered. They approached Reb Zalmen with good wishes for the soul of the departed, adding a prayer for long life for him and success in his business. But Itshele Kubats didn't forget who Reb Zalmen was, and he suddenly called out: "Zalmen, just tell me—who are you saying kaddish for today?"

Reb Zalmen didn't know what to do. He pulled himself together and said: "What difference does it make. Have another drink!"

As the crowd started getting up and getting ready to leave, Reb Zalmen suddenly broke out in a dance. It was the strangest thing—someone dancing in the Aleksander shtibl on his relative's yortsayt! And even stranger, Reb Zalmen himself never danced, not even on a holiday. When everyone used to gather in the shtibl or at someone's house to drink wine and they all started dancing, Reb Zalmen sat by himself and absolutely refused to join in. And even when the Hasidim tried to force him to join them, he would get angry and resist.

Reb Zalmen was against enthusiasm and hated the loss of self-control. True, anger could make him lose control, but not joy. Reb Zalmen used to say "anger is something you have to throw away from yourself. That is—you have to throw away both yourself, and the anger. But joy, that's something internal, something you have to keep inside yourself, especially since there's so little of it in the world."

And here was Reb Zalmen dancing. He danced as if possessed. No one could tell if he was drunk or sober. He kept on dancing, and no one could tell what was going on with him.

Reb Zalmen finished his dance. As if nothing special had just happened, he lifted his velvet hat with his left hand, took his velvet yarmulke in his right hand, wiped his close-shorn head, placed the hat back on his head, said "Good Shabbos!", put on his coat and walked home with my father for lunch.

Everybody in the shtibl could see that Reb Zalmen had handed out all of the stock in his "tavern." Somehow they knew that Reb Zalmen wouldn't be handing out any more liquor and snacks. This time they didn't leave one by one. Instead they walked away from the shtibl in groups, as they did every time something unusual happened in the shtibl.

Little Itshele Kubats, the Hasidic trickster, hurried from one group to the next, insisting: "Jews! It wasn't true! Zalmen didn't have yortsayt after all ... He was saying kaddish for his tavern ..."

And indeed, that was the end of Reb Zalmen's business.

CHAPTER SEVEN

Reb Zalmen at a Strange Table

For years Reb Zalmen had been our regular guest. Every Friday evening and every Shabbos morning he sat at the table with us. He came with Shabbos and when it finished he was gone. Sometimes he would drop in during the week as well, but only when he desperately needed a half zloty, or a shirt to take into the mikveh.

My father, my mother, and all of us children were so used to Reb Zalmen that we couldn't imagine a Shabbos or holiday meal without him. I can't remember even one such meal where he wasn't with us, except on Passover, when he would always travel to Aleksander to be with the Rebbe. If Reb Zalmen ever got sick, somehow by Shabbos or the holiday he would always get better.

Reb Zalmen enjoyed the generous servings at our home. Short, bent, shriveled Reb Zalmen, who got by on almost nothing all week, did enjoy his food on Shabbos. He liked my mother's egg challah, baked in our oven at home. When he took the bread knife inlaid with mother of pearl and engraved with the words "the holy Sabbath" and began to slice the shiny brown crust of the woven challah, he took pleasure in the moment. Except for fish and meat nothing was portioned out—he could take as much as he wanted. Whether it was honey cake or cookies on Shabbos morning, herring or sprats, or a portion of cholent, no one kept track of how much Zalmen was taking.

Best of all he liked the holiday feasts, when he could smoke a cigarette after eating, or before the tzimmes or compote. Reb Zalmen loved to smoke, and the stronger the cigarette the better. Every holiday I would buy a pack of Egyptians and give it to him while we were eating. Reb Zalmen would hide the gift in his pocket and take some of my father's cigarettes at the table.

And thus Reb Zalmen would be with us all year round—almost.

Almost, because before the High Holidays, when my father would take a vacation for four to six weeks and head to the spas, Reb Zalmen didn't eat at our home.

I was the only boy, and when my father left home I was the only male at home. I was still quite young then, and there was no way Reb Zalmen wanted to stay with me as the head of a "women's table," along with my mother, my five sisters and quite often one of their fellow students. No matter how much Reb Zalmen liked being with us the rest of the year, during this season he called it "the women's section." Overall his attitude toward women was dismissive. I don't remember him ever acknowledging my mother once during the years he ate with us, not even the way other Hasidim would address someone's wife: "Reb Itshe-Mayer's wife, the shtrudel is heavenly," or "Reb Itshe-Mayer's wife, how is your health?" Reb Zalmen knew that my mother was strictly observant, pious and indeed a Hasid in her own right. But as far as Reb Zalmen was concerned, that was no reason to soften the harsh light in which he judged all women.

From time to time we would be joined at the table by a young, Hasidic but somewhat modern couple. Reb Zalmen laughed right in the husband's face when he saw that the man let his wife go in front of him. He would say to me quietly, but loudly enough for everyone to hear: "Khil, that young man must be quite an ignoramus. You know why? Because the

Talmud comments on the verse in Judges 'And Manoach went after his wife,' 'Manoach was unlearned.' And that's precisely because he let his wife go in front of him."

Naturally that created an awkward situation. The young man blushed in shame. My sisters didn't understand what Reb Zalmen was saying, but they sensed that here he was insulting someone again. They were thoroughly annoyed by this "bizarre" Jew. Even my father, who in the end was satisfied with the rebuke of the young man, felt quite uncomfortable with this situation.

The only one whom it didn't bother, in fact, was Reb Zalmen himself. It didn't matter to him whether the young man felt insulted or not, whether my sisters liked him or not. He did what he had to do, and that's what gave him satisfaction.

Reb Zalmen would often repeat to me Hasidic and general sayings that denigrated women. Somehow putting women down gave him extraordinary pleasure. It seemed as though a secret desire to take revenge on them burned inside him. He didn't even want to hear about rebbes who accepted requests and contributions from women. He would wave his hands as if to dismiss them entirely. And that applied not only to the rebbes of his own day, but to the great *tsadikim* of the past as well.

Sometimes this pained my mother greatly. My mother's mother, Grandma Brayndl, was a passionate Porisover Hasid, who used to travel regularly to see the Rebbe Reb Yankev Hersh. It wasn't just an excursion, but a real journey to visit the Rebbe, with passion and commitment. During the month of Elul groups of women who were Porisover Hasidim got together. They rented ladder wagons from peasants, put down fresh straw, topped the straw with colorful kerchiefs, and along the roads of Poland, through orchards and fields, from Novominsk through Shenitse, Latavitsh and Sardin, they made their way to Porisov, drumming like the Prophet Miriam the whole way. My Grandma Brayndl went to see the Rebbe Reb Yankev Hersh not only in Elul, but even more often. At every opportunity—if there was a happy occasion or God forbid some trouble came up and her heart was heavy—she set straight off for Porisov. She was deeply respected at the Rebbe's court.

But that was all a long time ago, decades before we had met Reb Zalmen. The Rebbe Reb Yankev Hersh had already gone to the True World. My grandmother was no longer alive either. But that didn't hinder Zalmen, in his bitter enmity to women, from impugning the honor of such a saint as the Porisover and giving no quarter to my mother's feelings or the memory of her own deceased mother.

Occasionally my mother would very delicately hint to Reb Zalmen that his behavior pained her. My mother was very good to Reb Zalmen. She would often give him a larger portion than she did to the children. She would discreetly dish out a bit more, so that none of the children would notice and Reb Zalmen himself wouldn't feel insulted. She knew which of the dishes he liked best and would often hand him a treat. She didn't mind if I sometimes handed Reb Zalmen my white handkerchief if I noticed that he didn't have one and was forced to wipe his nose on his sleeve, or try to reach the hem of his satin caftan. On the contrary, my mother was pleased that I did that. But Reb Zalmen didn't see any of this. He was blind to everything. There was no way to bribe him or win him over when it came to women.

My father, who also didn't think much of rebbes who saw women, was nevertheless on my mother's side when it came to Porisov. And even though he didn't like repeating himself, in order to encourage her and make her feel better, he would often relate the story of what he had personally seen and heard in Porisov, in the company of the Rebbe Reb Yankev Hersh of blessed memory.

This was the story my father told:

"I was still a young man at that time," my father would calmly begin. "I was still studying and being supported by my father-in-law. At that time your Aunt Khane-Fayge, as your father told us children, was having a difficult labor, even though it was her third child. The labor went on for three days. Doctors in, doctors out. They sent all the way to Warsaw for a doctor. We were afraid she was about to die. Your grandmother approached me and asked me to go to Porisov, to the Rebbe Reb Yankev Hersh, even though I was an Aleksander Hasid myself. Of course I didn't refuse her, and I set off immediately.

"I reached Porisov in the morning, right after the morning prayers. The Rebbe was in his office already. He was immediately told who had come, and a minute later I was accompanied into his room.

"The Rebbe was still wearing his tallis and tefillin. He looked at me calmly, even though he clearly understood that I had come in response to some serious trouble. On the clear skin of his face, yellow-green like an esrog and covered with a thick white beard, not the least hint of distress could be seen. He sat in an armchair and shook my hand. I placed a note in his hand with my request.

"But even before the rebbe began reading the note, he opened his eyes, looked at me and asked, 'First of all, tell me how your mother-in-law is doing?'

"This frightened me a bit, because it's well known that when a rebbe asks you about someone else while you're handing him a note about a sick person, it's—God forbid—not a good sign. Nevertheless somehow I pulled myself together and answered, 'She is weak, as always.' Indeed, your grandmother was weak and delicate from her youth," my father explained.

"The Rebbe gave me a sharp look," my father continued, "and said to me in a strict, almost angry tone: 'You should tell your mother-in-law in my name, that for God's sake she should eat before she prays. I will take responsibility for her sin on myself.'"

With that, my father, my mother, and all of us children turned to Reb Zalmen with a triumphant look. You see the kind of grandmother we had! It's no small thing—the Porisover Rebbe, that great tsadik, took upon himself the sin to allow her to eat before praying. Ha! But Reb Zalmen remained unimpressed.

He sat on his side, avoided looking at the women's end of the table, and laughed to himself.

My sisters spoke only Polish amongst themselves and didn't know a word of Hebrew, but they'd heard the stories so many times that they understood the phrases my father used to mean "a difficult labor" or "mortal danger" and were familiar with the style of a Hasidic story. The elder of them didn't have any respect left for rebbes, for written requests and other kinds of "superstition," and even though the younger of them didn't yet know what going into labor meant or why one might need doctors for it, to spite Reb Zalmen they created a popular front, all the way from my father to my youngest sister, who was still a child at the time.

My father saw that Reb Zalmen wasn't terribly impressed by the story. In order to make more of an impression, without prompting my father further related the miracle he had personally seen when he was with the Rebbe Reb Yankev Hersh Tomashover.

He told us:

"As soon as the Rebbe read over the note I handed to him, he ordered brandy and honey cake to be brought so we could make a toast. After we drank, the Rebbe got up, went to the iron chest in his office and took out a bottle. He handed me the bottle and said the following words: 'Travel in good health, and travel now. As soon as you get home, see to it that this olive oil is smeared all over Yoysef-Leyb's body.' (Yoysef-Leyb was our uncle, my mother's only brother.)

"When I got home," my father concluded, "Khane-Fayge had been delivered of a son, and Yoysef-Leyb was consumed by fever. He was suffering from typhus. They smeared the oil all over him, and of course he got better."

At that point Reb Zalmen could no longer sit still. Something kept him out of his chair. He kept jumping up as though he were trying to shake off some noisome creature. Bits of words like little chips of wood came out of his mouth, and no one understood what he was saying. He put his hand on his head and rubbed his forehead with his yarmulke so hard that it looked like he was going mad. The story about the miracle really seemed to drive him crazy. It was a pity to watch him, and my father quickly changed the subject.

You can well understand that it wasn't easy to sit at the table with a Reb Zalmen like that. It took some time, but eventually all of us grew tired of him. The women in our family needed a rest. Indeed, perhaps my sisters were quite pleased that he wouldn't be joining us for a while. True, when it was still the first year that he was our regular guest and he told us he wouldn't be joining us while my father was out of town, we tried to dissuade him. We insisted that he should come anyway. As far as we were concerned, he was at home at our table, and it troubled us to think of him going anywhere else. But Reb Zalmen would not be dissuaded. Even more, he tried to convince me that I shouldn't eat at home while my father was away. Go to a restaurant if you have to, but don't sit down at the table with so many women. "They'll completely outnumber you," he argued. I was somewhat attracted to the idea. I was impressed by his project of becoming suddenly independent and going to eat at a restaurant. But my mother, my sisters, and my father were dead set against the idea. They thought the whole notion made no sense. Of course I stayed home for Shabbos and ate with my mother and sisters. But Reb Zalmen stuck to his guns, and for a short time stayed away from us.

Every year, before my father set off for the spa, he would arrange somewhere for Reb Zalmen to eat on Shabbos. He would choose a wealthy and generous household, where no guest would feel slighted, and where he knew Reb Zalmen would feel comfortable. It wasn't easy to find that sort of place for Reb Zalmen. He was a difficult person and easily offended. And on the other hand not everybody was willing to have him as a guest. He was known to be stubborn and angry. Everybody, but especially rich people, likes to have things quiet and orderly at mealtime, and it wasn't always that way when Reb Zalmen was around. You never knew what was going to happen.

People who didn't know him well found it difficult to get along with him. Yet someone was always willing to have him when my father was away.

One year Reb Shmuel, the owner of the building in which we lived, came to my father and said that he'd be quite willing to have Reb Zalmen as a guest while my father was away. My father was starting to prepare for the trip and had in mind to look for a place for Reb Zalmen. Reb Shmuel was also an Aleksander Hasid and prayed in the same shtibl as my father and Reb Zalmen. He was quite wealthy. He was one of the best-known commercial paper dealers in Warsaw and owned several buildings.

Nevertheless my father wasn't really happy with Reb Shmuel's offer. True, he was an Aleksander Hasid, but he never went to see the Rebbe. When the Rebbe himself came to Warsaw, Reb Shmuel would go to see him, but he never made the journey himself. And his home was closed to others. He would never invite a crowd of Hasidim to come for kiddush. And on the rare occasions when he did provide kiddush at home, he would only invite selected individuals whom he knew very well. He had several young adult daughters at home, and he seemed in no hurry to marry them off, even though he had plenty of money to do so. They said that his wife was far from easyoing.

On a personal level my father was indifferent to Reb Shmuel. When he spoke of Reb Shmuel he used a Polish saying that translates, "He doesn't smell nice and he doesn't stink either." On the other hand, my father thoroughly disliked Reb Shmuel's home. It lacked the least bit of Hasidic warmth. Somehow the place was melancholy, as though the home itself suffered from a diseased liver.

Yet my father couldn't refuse Reb Shmuel. We'd lived in the same house for over ten years. We weren't close, but we behaved properly toward one another. It's hard to say "No." My father promised to talk it over with Reb Zalmen.

To this day it's hard for me to comprehend exactly why Reb Shmuel wanted to have Reb Zalmen as a guest. Emotional and turbulent Reb Zalmen was hardly a good fit for Reb Shmuel's cold and stiff household. I imagine that Reb Shmuel thought it would be fun to see the reaction of his wife and his free-thinking daughters to Reb Zalmen. The eldest daughter was a student at Warsaw University and thought her father was an old-fashioned Hasidic zealot.

But Reb Zalmen was no shrinking violet. When my father explained that Reb Shmuel, our landlord, wanted to have him as a guest, he didn't pay any attention to my father's hesitations and immediately said, "Yes. Well, we'll see. How bad could it be? If he wants me, I'll come."

One Friday night after my father had left, Reb Zalmen set off to Reb Shmuel's house for the first time. Reb Shmuel didn't go to the shtibl on Friday nights. Instead he prayed at home on his own. He didn't want to take the trouble to go to the shtibl for the short Friday evening service, just as he didn't want to deal in small amounts of commercial paper. So Reb Zalmen went to the Friday night meal by himself. He knocked on Reb Shmuel's door for a long time. They didn't open the door there as readily as at our home, where my father didn't even have to knock because everybody was waiting for him to come home and heard his footsteps outside. At Reb Shmuel's you had to knock and keep on knocking. Standing outside the door Reb Zalmen began to feel a bit discouraged. He knocked again, and eventually heard a voice: "*Kto tam?*" (Who's there, in Polish.) At first Reb Zalmen didn't understand what was going on, and when he did he shouted loudly: "Me! Me!" A dark, heavy door, secured with a chain, opened a crack. Through the narrow opening appeared the laughing eyes of a servant girl in a short white apron. She gave the hunched-over Reb Zalmen a cheerful glance. The door closed again and Reb Zalmen continued to stand waiting outside. He was getting ready to go, but suddenly he heard the clink of the chain, the door opened and the same smiling young servant girl let Zalmen into a long, barely-lit corridor.

Reb Zalmen stood in the semi-dark hallway with the girl. He became terrified. Reb Zalmen, who used to dismiss all the women in the world with a wave of his hand, who on account of his contempt for women had abandoned our home where we considered him part of the family, that same Reb Zalmen now realized that the young serving girl was laughing at him. He felt altogether out of place. He looked around to see if he could escape. He started to shuffle backwards toward the door. But in a commanding tone, the servant girl told him to take off his coat. He obeyed. She didn't let him hang up his coat on a hanger in the closet where the family's coats were. Instead she pointed him to a corner of the corridor where there was a box covering the gas meter. That's where she ordered him to put down his coat, and again he obeyed.

She opened the door to a small waiting room. The servant girl went in front, and Reb Zalmen followed her. From there she guided him into a brightly-lit dining room. She stayed in front, and he behind. He felt totally lost. Finally he spotted Reb Shmuel. Reb Zalmen breathed deeply and barely managed to stammer "Good Shabbos!"

Reb Shmuel sat in an armchair at a long table which was surrounded by tall, upholstered seats, in the middle of a large room whose walls were covered halfway up with dark paneling and then with thick, brown, heavy wallpaper. The back of his armchair was so high that Reb Shmuel was entirely hidden from the back. Even the hat on his head was invisible. Reb Zalmen had no choice but to follow the servant girl a bit further into the dining room before he spotted Reb Shmuel. The latter responded to Reb Zalmen's "Good Shabbos," and with a slow motion of his hand pointed to a seat on the left side of the table, between Reb Shmuel's two sons.

Reb Zalmen sat down and saw across the table a group of young women of marriageable age who stared at him in mocking curiosity. To his left and right he saw Reb Shmuel's two grown sons, both clean-shaven.

The hymn *Sholem-Aleykhem* that Reb Zalmen recited before kiddush didn't have the same quality as it did at our home, where he sat in comfort and swayed left and right during the recitation. Now he was squeezed between the two young men. If he turned right he bumped into one beardless person, and if he turned left he bumped into the other. He felt claustrophobic. He made kiddush with the melody of the Aleksander Hasidim and in their style, loud and enunciating every word. His kiddush did make some impression and evoked some respect for him. But when it came to the song *Azamer beshvokhin* and Reb Zalmen tried to use the Vurker Hasidim's melody, clapping along with his hands, he saw the mockery in Reb Shmuel's daughters' eyes, and behind his back he sensed that the two young men were mocking him with their hands.

Then the food was brought in. On Friday night, when the platters were full of meat and fish, when there was plenty of chicken broth and plenty inside of it as well, Reb Zalmen was able to eat enough, even if not more than that as he was used to getting.

Shabbos morning, when Reb Zalmen came from the shtibl and sat down to make kiddush, he looked for the bottle of alcohol. He always made kiddush on a cup of pure alcohol. Reb Zalmen preferred to pour the liquor directly from a bottle. He didn't trust a carafe. But there was no bottle on the table. Instead he saw a round carafe with some light yellow liquid, on the bottom of which swam bits of lemon peel.

Reb Zalmen asked what it was. They told him that it was diluted brandy. As far as Reb Zalmen was concerned, watered liquor was worse than mixing linen and wool. He asked whether there might be a bit of undiluted liquor in the house. Reb Shmuel answered that he didn't keep it in the house; as soon as he bought a bottle, he added water. Reb Zalmen didn't know what to do, but since he didn't have a choice he made kiddush on the diluted brandy. He thought for a moment about which blessing to make first, the one over the drink or the one over the baked goods. When he had straight liquor the answer was always clear: it was always more important than even the best pastries. Out of sheer habit, he recited the *shehakol* blessing first this time as well. He poured the diluted liquor into his mouth like a dose of bitter medicine. Liquor he would drink slowly, not like most people. I had often noticed how Reb Zalmen would pour the liquor onto his gums and keep it in his mouth, and it didn't seem to bother him at all. Apparently his gums were already scorched, accustomed to the liquor. Now, when he'd poured the diluted brandy into his throat, he wanted a bit of something. But he didn't see a bowl of honey cake and cookies like at our home. On a small round plate near his seat lay three anise cookies, dark, evidently store bought. Reb Zalmen recited the *mazones* blessing and tried to break the cookie so he could put some of it in his mouth. But the cookie was so hard that he couldn't break it. He became angry with the stingy rich man who couldn't bother to have something baked at home even for the kiddush. With his weak teeth he barely managed to bite off a bit of the cookie and dipped it in brandy, to avoid having made a blessing over nothing at all. He began to regret the whole business and was sorry he'd agreed to go to Reb Shmuel.

Reb Zalmen was invited to go wash his hands. He approached the washing stand that stood in the corner of the big dining room and poured two dippers of water over his hands. Suddenly he felt someone tugging at his sleeve. It was the cheerful serving girl, standing next to him and handing him a rough little hand towel, probably from the kitchen. He grew more and more annoyed. In his irritation he shouted the preliminary words "Raise your hands," and then the blessing on hand washing right in the servant girl's face. She immediately stopped smiling and started looking at this bizarre Jew with fearful curiosity. Reb Zalmen frowned and went to the table. The challah that had tasted fresh on Friday night now stuck to the roof of his mouth like clay. His tongue worked at the bit of bread inside his mouth until he could finally swallow it. He thought of my mother's braided challahs which shone yellow on Shabbos morning, the plump crusts looking like happy faces. He ate the store-bought challah as if it were a punishment. Then a long dish was set next to him. On the dish lay the head of a herring and one thin middle portion, along with some diced onion. Reb Zalmen wasn't used to getting a portion of herring. He became even angrier. He worked hard to contain himself. He ate the middle portion of the fish but didn't touch the head. Then Reb Zalmen reached out his hand for the carafe to take a glass of brandy. Even though he detested the diluted brandy, he was so angry he felt he absolutely had to have something to drink. But when he took the carafe of brandy without being invited everyone at the table was amazed. They weren't used to such a bold guest. Then the platter of fish was brought to the table, by now only half covered with full and partial pieces. The mistress of the house lingered over one plate. Then she set it down next to Reb Zalmen. Reb Zalmen saw on the plate a heap of carrots, pieces of cooked onion, bits of parsley, and on the very bottom the sad tail of a fish.

Reb Zalmen's face first turned red, then gray, then white as though he were fainting, and then back to yellow. With a trembling hand he pushed the plate away and began to murmur something.

Reb Shmuel thought that Reb Zalmen was reciting Sabbath hymns. He was surprised that Reb Zalmen simply said the hymn like a *misnaged* rather than singing them. But suddenly Reb Zalmen stood up, moved away from the table, went over to the washstand, poured water over the tips of his fingers, came back, sat at the table and began to recite the blessing after meals out loud by himself.

Reb Zalmen's loud recitation frightened Reb Shmuel. Everyone at the table was struck mute and breathless. Even the servant girl who happened to enter just then stood waiting to see what would happen next. Reb Zalmen took his time going through the blessings. His face was tightly drawn, his eyes closed, only the lips curled, as if they wanted to spit the words out of his mouth. When Reb Zalmen finally finished with the words "The Lord will bless His people in peace," he stood up and said to Reb Shmuel:

"Listen Shmuel, the Talmud says that Rebbe Yochanan and Rebbe Eliezer both said that as long as the Holy Temple stood the Altar removed the sins of the Jews, but now a man's table will take away his sins. Every Jewish table is an altar, and the guest is the sacrifice on that altar. So instead of me eating the tail of that fish and being the sacrifice for you, I think you should eat the tail and be the sacrifice for me ..."

And with that Reb Zalmen left the room and banged the door behind him.

Nobody knows what happened at Reb Shmuel's after Reb Zalmen left. Neighbors reported that during the meal they heard a loud crash as of breaking crockery. For quite some time afterward Reb Shmuel altogether avoided talking to my father, as if somehow he held my father responsible. And Reb Shmuel ran away from Reb Zalmen as if he were a demon. Nor did Reb Zalmen himself ever breathe a word about what had happened at Reb Shmuel's, or about what he had said before leaving. But one Purim, when Reb Zalmen was a bit high, I bribed him with two packs of "Egyptians" to tell me the story. We had a good laugh, and Reb Zalmen enjoyed exhaling from his mouth and nose the fragrant smoke of the cigarettes that he had earned fair and square.

CHAPTER EIGHT

The Handshake

1.

Suddenly Reb Zalmen decided he wanted money.

It's easy to say "he wanted it." This wasn't a casual whim, but some kind of mad lust for money that took over all of Reb Zalmen's thoughts and senses, wouldn't let him be for a moment, wouldn't let him rest. A violent desire consumed him like a tapeworm, no less urgent than the desire of a man for a woman.

It wasn't even clear to Reb Zalmen himself why he needed the money or what he would do with it. He didn't dream of being wealthy. He didn't picture himself as a rich man, how he would look, where he would live, what he would eat, how others would behave around him. No, Reb Zalmen didn't give a thought to any of that. It was simply the raw desire for money. The Evil Inclination took on the form of silver and golden pieces and lured Reb Zalmen night and day with their clinking sound and bright reflection.

Reb Zalmen walked around in a daze. He couldn't think straight. He would spend half a day wrapped in his tallis and tefillin and couldn't concentrate enough even to recite abridged morning prayers with the proper intent. He was thin enough already but now he shriveled like a prune. His red-rimmed eyes burned with a hellish fire. He'd never been easy to get along with, but now he became so cross that no one could stand him for a minute.

The crowd in the Aleksander shtibl where he spent his days and nights realized that something out of the ordinary was going on with him, but no one had a clue what it was. When any of the Hasidim tried to talk to Reb Zalmen about his condition, he became so angry that he cursed like a street hooligan.

Some of the Hasidim in the shtibl hinted at the fact that Reb Zalmen had no wife. But he was already seventy years old. No one remembered if he'd ever had a wife. And it didn't make sense that now, when he was an old man, he'd suddenly be overcome with lust.

Some of the Hasidim suggested that a spirit had possessed Reb Zalmen. There was no other way to understand his behavior, no other way to understand the change that had come over him. Hasidim who happened to visit the Aleksander Rebbe at that time mentioned Reb Zalmen to the Rebbe. But Reb Zalmen remained the same: he was still obsessed and wouldn't talk to anyone.

Reb Zalmen himself sensed that this whole business of money was the work of Satan. He clearly sensed that the lust for money would be his ruin. He felt worthless, as though he'd suddenly lost all of his spiritual attainments, become petty, yet he couldn't help himself.

The crowd in the shtibl were extremely eager to find out what was going on, and the most curious among them was Itshele Kubats. Itshele had always loved to tease Reb Zalmen, and he certainly didn't stop now. As soon as Itshele entered the shtibl, he went up to Reb Zalmen. And though Reb Zalmen tried to make him go away with a string of curses and formulas of banishment, Itshele stuck close, watching every step, listening to every word, following Reb Zalmen like his shadow.

One evening Reb Zalmen sat in the shtibl reciting Psalms in a broken voice. He'd taken up the practice recently. When he was by himself in the shtibl he recited Psalms just like the "middle" Aleksander Rebbe of blessed memory used to do. When that Rebbe would begin reciting Psalms to himself in his own room, he would put the book in his left hand, lower his right shoulder halfway down his tall, thin body, and in this bizarre and broken stance he would pace back and forth through the room reciting Psalms with such intensity that it would have moved a stone to hear it.

Reciting the Book of Psalms didn't demand that Reb Zalmen get into the right frame of mind. It led him along gently, like a child leading a blind person along a path strewn with obstacles. This particular day it was between minchah and maariv. There were people in the shtibl, so Reb Zalmen didn't pace back and forth. He sat at the table, reading.

He recited the section of Psalms designated to be recited on Shabbos. When Reb Zalmen reached Psalm 115 and the phrase, "Their idols are silver and gold," he couldn't move past the words "silver and gold." He repeated them dozens of times: "silver and gold ... silver and gold ..." without stopping, as if sinking in quicksand.

Little Itshele Kubats, who'd been sitting quietly behind Reb Zalmen's back the whole time, jumped up like a cat, stood up on the tips of his toes like demon and shouted right in Reb Zalmen's face: "Listen, Zalmen! What's got you stuck on the silver and gold of those idols? Zalmen, forget about the silver and gold. What's with you, Zalmen?"

Reb Zalmen stood up. His shriveled face suddenly looked like a rehydrated mushroom. He raised his fisted hands, stared at Itshele and shouted: "Money can make a bastard kosher, and it can certainly do the same for a Hasid! I want money, money, money!"

The crowd looked at Reb Zalmen as if he'd lost his mind.

2.

By then everyone in the shtibl knew that Reb Zalmen had been overcome with desire for money. Money was the main topic of their conversations. And the paupers talked about it more than anyone.

They repeated over and over the story about Reb Mendl of Kotsk, who'd said to his Rebbe Reb Bunem: "Money? Feh!"

And the Rebbe Reb Bunem later related that after he'd heard those words, he didn't want to touch a coin for thirty days. People talked about the attitude toward money of figures such as the Seer of Lublin and the Maggid of Kozhenits. It was said that the Seer used to make his wealthy Hasidim promise that if they happened to go through Kozhenits, they mustn't try to visit the Maggid, because with one dismissive wave of his hand he could ruin them financially, as had happened more than once already. They talked about the difference between Reb Nokhem of Chernobl and Reb Motele: the father, Reb Nokhem, valued poverty while his son Reb Motele valued wealth. They talked about the manners of the sons of the Rizhiner, who acted like nobility.

The more "worldly" Hasidim told stories about Jan Bloch, about Meir Anshl Rothschild and the "Prince," Reb Moshe Montefiore.

But all of this talk about money in the shtibl didn't change a thing for Reb Zalmen. He didn't even listen to it. He grew thinner by the day. He was flickering like a candle.

But how could Reb Zalmen have had any money? He wasn't a manufacturer, he wasn't a merchant, he wasn't even a broker. He had nothing to do with making money at all.

A few of the Hasidim raised a couple of rubles and advised Reb Zalmen to buy a lottery ticket. Maybe his number would come up. And even if he didn't win the grand prize, he might still win something. If Reb Zalmen was so obsessed with money, there must be something to it.

But Reb Zalmen wouldn't hear of such a thing. He was terribly suspicious by nature. He didn't trust anyone. It wasn't only that he didn't want to trust the Jewish lotteries run at the various Hasidic courtyards, such as Ger, Aleksander, Lublin, or Pilts, or the lotteries run by Handelsman or Mikhl Elye—he didn't even trust the Russian Tsar with the few rubles it would cost to get a ticket.

Things had come to a desperate state, may we be preserved …

Until once, while reciting Psalms, Reb Zalmen had a thought. His face lit up. The simplicity of his idea left him stunned and amazed. He couldn't understand why he hadn't thought of it earlier. He couldn't forgive himself for taking so long.

It was the simplest of ideas. Reb Zalmen decided to become a *shadkhn*, a marriage broker. A shadkhn doesn't need any capital, just some good sense and some luck. One side has to have the girl, the other—the boy. One side needs to have a large dowry, the other—something less. One side has to be able to provide gifts for the bride, the other—gifts for the groom. But the shadkhn doesn't need to have anything except a bit of brains and a drop of luck. The brains Reb Zalmen had, he could rely on that. Luck? That's up to Heaven, it requires total faith in God. And faith was something Reb Zalmen had plenty of.

3.

And that's how Reb Zalmen became a shadkhn. My father had a collection of walking sticks which he treasured. He guarded it carefully and made sure from time to time to add a new item with distinctive decoration, a special handle or a heavy band at the top. He gave Reb Zalmen a black stick. My mother gave Reb Zalmen several handkerchiefs, and our servant girl Genendl polished his coat, which had once been black, with a whole jar of blacking.

One bright morning Reb Zalmen started knocking on the doors of Hasidic homes to propose matches.

Reb Zalmen was welcomed everywhere. He was given a bite to eat, but he didn't want to touch the food until he had time to explain exactly why he had come. He cited the example of Abraham's servant. When the latter wanted to propose to Laban and Besuel that Laban's daughter Rachel, whom the servant had just met at the well in Padam Aram, should marry Abraham's son Isaac, he said "I won't eat until I've said my piece."

Everyone listened to Reb Zalmen respectfully and intently. They promised right away to consider carefully the match he'd proposed. Once he'd gotten that reassurance Reb Zalmen would eat with a good appetite the snacks he was offered.

But when Reb Zalmen returned to find out where things stood with the proposed match, either the master of the house wasn't home or the mistress was away. In the latter case the husband would say that he hadn't yet had a chance to discuss the matter with his wife and couldn't give Reb Zalmen a definite answer one way or the other. Reb Zalmen was still offered a snack, but not as generously as the first time. Sometimes he was merely offered a glass of tea.

When Reb Zalmen became insistent, coming back time after time, starting to show that he was getting annoyed, neither the husband nor the wife would talk to him. Instead, the servant girl would tell Reb Zalmen that her masters weren't home. If Reb Zalmen resisted leaving and sat to wait, the next time the servant girl refused to let him in the door.

Reb Zalmen was beside himself. He could tell people were avoiding him. He could tell he wasn't making it as a shadkhn. But for the life of him he couldn't understand why. At first when he tried out matchmaking he tried his best to become more accommodating and relaxed. Now he became so angry and unpleasant that even Reb Leybl, another Aleksander Hasid who prayed in the same shtibl as Reb Zalmen and was always looking to do another Hasid a favor, who greeted everyone with a smiling "Good morning" and an even warmer "Good Shabbos," who held out both hands to shake, no longer had patience for Reb Zalmen.

Although Reb Zalmen himself didn't know why he wasn't being accepted as a shadkhn, the other Hasidim in the Aleksander shtibl remembered a story from years before, which was enough to ruin his new profession.

This was back in the time when the big Aleksander shtibl in Warsaw was on Nalewki Street. In the same courtyard as the shtibl lived a Jew named Avrem Borekh. He was somewhat wealthy and somewhat sickly, and he owned half of a building in the better part of Warsaw. Once upon a time Avrem Borekh had been a Naradzhiner Hasid. But since he'd become an invalid he'd stopped making pilgrimages to see any rebbe. But when the Aleksander Rebbe or one of the grandsons of the Vurke Rebbe came to Warsaw, Reb Avrem Borekh would go to see him and hand him a note with a request and a donation, not the way a Hasid does, but like an ordinary member of the community.

Reb Avrem Borekh had never been much of a scholar, nor had he ever been a particularly devoted Hasid. He was by nature quiet and reserved. He never raised his voice. It was said in his later years that even as a youngster he'd had a delicate constitution.

Reb Avrem Borekh had a short, thin wife who was even quieter than he was. They had a single daughter. They had never had any other children.

Doctors and—no comparison intended—rebbes had cost him the value of half his house, leaving him with just the other half, but nothing had resulted in a son.

Reb Avrem Borekh's daughter was of middle height, with white hands and a forehead white as snow. She had deep black eyes and hair black as pitch. She was a charming Jewish girl. She always sat home sewing at an embroidery frame.

When she matured and Reb Avrem Borekh needed a match for his only daughter, the search began in earnest. Reb Avrem Borekh didn't care about money or status. All he wanted was a scholarly son-in-law.

And even though there was no shortage of learned young men in Warsaw or anywhere in Russian Poland at that time, somehow Reb Avrem Borekh didn't manage to find one that suited him. Since he wasn't so learned himself, he was terribly afraid of being deceived. He dreaded ignorant Jews. He couldn't forget the passage in the Tractate Pesachim: "Whoever marries his daughter to an ignoramus, it's as if he tied her up and placed her in front of a lion. Just as a lion tears flesh and gobbles without shame, so too an ignoramus beats his wife and takes her without shame." The very thought of it made him uneasy. He vividly pictured himself in his mind bringing his own gentle daughter and placing her before a lion to be torn, God forbid, in pieces. He couldn't sleep at night, and when he did fall asleep, he had miserable nightmares. In his dreams he saw his son-in-law abusing his daughter in bed. It was enough to make his hair stand on end. He would wake up shouting and covered in cold sweat.

As far as Reb Avrem Borekh was concerned, it would have been better for his daughter to remain an old maid than to see her married off to an ignoramus.

Reb Avrem Borekh's wife tried to reassure her husband. "What's the problem?" she argued. "If you want to find a scholar, who's going to deceive you? What do you think the world has come to? Is there any lack of scholarly young men? Since you're not looking for money, but you don't want an orphan either, what could be easier than taking a trip to a yeshiva and asking the head of the yeshiva to show you the finest young man, and then make him our son-in-law?"

On the other hand, even though Reb Avrem Borekh didn't care much about money, he didn't want to make a match with a poor family either. He wouldn't have cared much himself, but he considered it beneath his daughter's dignity and he saw no reason why it should be necessary.

So Reb Avrem Borekh had no choice but to deal with shadkhanim, and they in turn sparked his mistrust. Being himself a scrupulously honest man, Reb Avrem Borekh was very sensitive to falsehood. Every time a shadkhn used imprecise language it made him nervous. The shadkhanim's pitches weren't only imprecise; very often they contained outright lies. Reb Avrem Borekh grew more and more suspicious. He stopped believing the shadkhanim even when everyone else confirmed their reports. A number of times a proposed match was on the verge of being concluded. But at the last minute Reb Avrem Borekh would start dragging the matter out, arguing about every detail, holding off on giving a definite answer, until the prospective in-laws got insulted and the whole matter came to naught. And even though at the time it seemed that Reb Avrem

Borekh was bitterly disappointed, the truth was that he was greatly relieved.

Shadkhanim came and went. There wasn't a single Talmud student in Poland from a semi-respectable family who hadn't been proposed as a match for his daughter, and matches were proposed for her beyond Poland as well, in Frankfurt am Mein and Amsterdam. But Reb Avrem Borekh could never commit himself.

The shadkhanim became impatient. They were openly annoyed at Reb Avrem Borekh. They pointed out that with just half a house, even in the "finer streets," Reb Avrem Borekh wasn't such a big shot. They let him know that his poor health also wasn't exactly a selling point. More than once they hinted that he shouldn't think that he was the only one who had to make up his mind, and that the prospective mother-in-law wanted to take the girl to be examined by a doctor before the deal was concluded …

All of these hints and warnings made Reb Avrem Borekh even more suspicious, more bitter, more stubborn. He noticed that the shadkhanim stopped coming. He learned that whenever someone suggested to a parent a match with Reb Avrem Borekh's daughter, the suggestion was immediately dismissed. He looked at his refined, lovely daughter with a heavy heart, but he didn't know what else to do.

4

And then one fine day before the High Holidays, a provincial shadkhn approached Reb Avrem Borekh and proposed a match with the son of a Jew from Ozorkov, a sock manufacturer and an Aleksander Hasid.

Until the day he died Reb Avrem Borekh could not quite figure out why this particular match seemed promising to him. Somehow right away he had the sense that something would come out of this proposal.

However, Reb Avrem Borekh's poor health didn't permit him to travel to Ozerkov, and he didn't like the idea of sending someone to test the youngster without Reb Avrom Borkeh being present. On the other hand, the boy's father absolutely refused to travel to Warsaw so that the boy could be examined there. Reb Avrem Borekh wanted the match to go through, and he kept trying to figure out how to make it happen.

As mentioned, Reb Avrem Borekh lived in part of a building where the Aleksander shtibl had once stood. He prayed there and became close to Reb Zalmen.

Although Reb Zalmen disdained Reb Avrem Borekh, didn't want to be closely associated with him, and certainly wasn't impressed by Reb Avrem Borekh's wealth, Reb Avrem Borekh still kept after Reb Zalmen. He often invited Reb Zalmen to his home. The quiet and reserved Reb Avrem Borekh absolutely enjoyed Reb Zalmen's sharp sayings and insults of others.

Now, when the proposed match with the boy from Ozorkov came up, Reb Avrem Borekh had the idea that Reb Zalmen was someone he could trust to test the lad. He knew that Reb Zalmen wouldn't give in to anybody. He knew how much Reb Zalmen hated ignorance, so he decided that since there was no other choice, he would trust Reb Zalmen's judgment.

And Reb Avrem Borekh didn't hesitate for a minute. He went into the shtibl and said to Reb Zalmen: "Listen, Reb Zalmen, you've probably heard about how hard a time I've had finding a match for my daughter. She is an only child. I'm terribly afraid of winding up with a son-in-law who's an ignoramus. Now somebody's proposing a match with a boy from Ozorkov. I don't even know why myself, but I like this match. Since I can't travel to Ozorkov to test the boy, I have a favor to ask of you, Reb Zalmen. Since you're headed to Aleksander for the High Holidays and the man from Ozorkov and his son will also be with the Rebbe, I'm going to ask you to do me a favor and carefully test the boy. I can rely on you, Reb Zalmen, but for God's sake please don't forget!"

"Avrem Borekh, you can rely on me. If I say it's a test, that's what it is! I'll take that boy out on the carpet, and believe me, I'll find out what he knows and what he doesn't know."

Reb Zalmen and Reb Avrem Borekh didn't think anything further need be said about the arrangement.

When Reb Zalmen arrived in Aleksander before Rosh Hashanah, everything was confusion. The town was full of Hasidim. All of the inns were completely occupied. The hotel keepers mercilessly gouged the wealthier Hasidim. Reb Zalmen himself wasn't worried about finding a place to stay. He slept in the Rebbe's study house and ate at the Rebbe's table. But still it was Rosh Hashanah, with the lengthy services, the shofar blowing, the festive meals, handouts from the Rebbe's own plate, the Rebbe's discourses. With everything going on, Reb Zalmen completely forgot about the match.

Not until the day after Yom Kippur, when the crowd of Hasidim began to get ready to go home for Sukkos, did Reb Zalmen remember his promise to Avrem Borekh. Reb Zalmen began asking around, trying to locate the Jew from Ozorkov and his son. When he finally managed to do so, and arrived panting at their inn, it turned out that they had already set off for the marketplace so they could get in the coach and go home.

When Reb Zalmen came running into the marketplace dozens such coaches already stood in harness, filled with hundreds of Hasidim holding black leather satchels on their knees. Empty coaches made their way into the marketplace and full ones departed. Reb Zalmen barely managed to find out which coach was heading to Ozorkov. When he reached it, it was already overfull, and the coachman had to scramble up onto the box, where he was getting ready to set off.

Reb Zalmen immediately spotted the man from Ozorkov, distinguished by a wide, luxurious beard. Next to him sat a plump lad with round, rosy cheeks.

Reb Zalmen shouted up to the coach: "Listen, rich man from Ozorkov, Avrem Borekh from Warsaw made me promise to test your son. That he can eat, I see; but I want to know if he can learn like he can eat. Get down with your boy and we'll go into a tavern, and I can test him there."

"And where were you all this time, Zalmen? Ten days weren't enough for you, Zalmen? I'm not getting out of the coach. As far as I'm concerned, you don't have to test the boy. Chaskl!" he called to the coachman, "pick up the reins and take off."

Reb Zalmen didn't know what to do. Suddenly he realized what he'd done. He didn't know how he could show his face to Reb Borekh. And even more important—he didn't want to be the cause of a ruined match. Reb Zalmen, who was always decisive, was in a dilemma. Suddenly he had an idea, and turning to the lad with the round, rosy cheeks he asked:

"Listen, kid, do you know how to learn?"

"Yes," the boy answered, a bit embarrassed.

"Tell me, do you really know how to learn?"

"Yes."

"Don't just say 'yes,' say: 'I really know how to learn.'"

The boy said, "I really know how to learn."

"If so, shake my hand on it," and Reb Zalmen reached out his hand to the boy.

The boy looked at his father. His father answered with an angry look, and the boy reached out his hand to take Reb Zalmen's. At that moment the coach began to move.

Reb Zalmen stayed in Aleksander through all of Sukkos, and even when the holiday was over he wasn't in a rush to get "home." Reb Zalmen had no home. He lived in the shtibl, so what was the rush?

But he couldn't stay in Aleksander forever, either. Three weeks after the holiday ended, the Rebbe's wife gave him money for the trip, and he returned to Warsaw.

Reb Avrem Borekh anxiously waited for Reb Zalmen's return. Several times a day he went into the shtibl to find out if Reb Zalmen had gotten back yet. And when Reb Zalmen finally returned, Reb Avrem Borekh went into the shtibl, greeted him and asked, "Well?"

"Avrem Borekh, you have nothing to worry about. Not only does the boy know how to learn—he *really* knows how to learn." But when Reb Avrem Borekh wanted to hear more details, Reb Zalmen didn't have anything more to say.

The meeting to settle details of the match was arranged for a town between Warsaw and Ozorkov. The bride was showered with gifts. Reb Avrem Borekh and his wife were shown profound honor. It was like a major holiday. Although this part of the ceremony was the responsibility of the bride's side, the groom's family announced that since the bride's father was an invalid they would take care of everything. Reb Avrem Borekh was deeply impressed by his future in-law's decency and consideration.

Reb Avrem Borekh hoped to have a conversation with the groom, but the latter said almost nothing. His father hinted to Reb Avrem Borekh that the boy was easily embarrassed, and that such sensitivity was a fine character trait for a Jew …

During the year of the engagement Reb Avrem Borekh sent the groom a full set of the Vilan edition of the Talmud, Maimonides' Mishneh Torah, and other scholarly books. The groom would send written analyses on various topics to his father-in-law. Reb Zalmen read these over, and although in general he didn't like such picayune analyses, these pleased him, because they confirmed that he was right about the boy.

The wedding was in Warsaw. During the meal after the ceremony the groom delivered a Torah analysis which somehow didn't please Reb Avrem Borekh. Somehow the boy was speaking too mechanically. But it was a lavish wedding, everyone had had a few drinks, and almost nobody paid attention while the boy was talking. Only Reb Avrem Borekh, the single sober person at his only daughter's wedding, felt a stab in his heart …

After the wedding it became clear that Reb Avrem Borekh's son-in-law was a total boor, a classic ignoramus. It was simply incomprehensible how a Jew could be so ignorant.

Reb Avrem Borekh felt like he was the guilty one. He felt like the walls were closing in on him. "What I feared has come to pass," he said to himself in the words of Job. He almost died of anguish.

Reb Avrem Borekh's son-in-law did remember one brief passage in the Talmud: "Rav Safra used to singe the head of the animal (before it was cooked for Shabbos); Rava would salt the shibuta fish." Salted the fish! With that the young man ran into the kitchen to put salt on the fish, embarrassing the servant girl.

Reb Avrem Borekh began insisting that his daughter get a divorce, but she wept bitterly. The marriage was a disaster, falling on her head like a cloudburst. She was frightened and discouraged. And now she should display her shame in public? "I'd rather die than get divorced," she complained to her father.

Time passed, and when Reb Avrem Borekh continued to tell his daughter she should get a divorce, his wife whispered to him that the young woman was expecting.

Reb Avrem Borekh began to avoid company. He stopped coming into the Aleksander shtibl. But one time he decided to venture out, and when he discovered that Reb Zalmen was alone in the shtibl, he went up to Reb Zalmen and said with his hands balled into fists: "Zalmen, you murderer! You robber! You killer! You slaughtered me without a knife. You're going to have to pay for this sooner or later. What did you have against me? Why did I deserve this?"

Reb Zalmen's red-rimmed eyes opened wide. "Are you out of your mind? Avrem Borekh! Who are you talking about?"

"You! Nobody else! You tested my son-in-law and told me that he knows to learn, and he turned out to be a complete fool, an utter ignoramus!"

Reb Zalmen went pale as chalk. His small, bent body collapsed further and became half again smaller. He trembled all over. Suddenly his eyes became fiery. His face turned from white to red. He stood up on the tips of his toes and in a hoarse voice angrily shouted: "What, he doesn't know how to learn? You should know that he isn't just an ignoramus, but a miserable sinner as well!"

"???!!!"

"We shook hands on it. He lied to me!"

The story about how Reb Zalmen had "tested" Reb Avrem Borekh's son-in-law had to come out. No matter how much Reb Avrem Borekh tried, he couldn't hide his son-in-law's ignorance for very long. The whole Hasidic world couldn't stop repeating the story of how Reb Zalmen had "tested" the young man.

Years had passed. Reb Avrem Borekh had died years before. The son-in-law, whose wife bore him a dozen children, became very wealthy, and bought back the other half of the house, which his father-in-law had sold off to pay for doctors and rebbes in hopes of getting the son he never had.

A new generation grew up. Even respectable Hasidim flattered Reb Avrem Borekh's rich son-in-law. Everyone forgot about the handshake, and the elderly Reb Zalmen, whose memory was failing by now in any case, forgot about the episode altogether. Not until Reb Zalmen tried to become a shadkhn did people remember about the handshake. And although years had since gone by and the world had changed in many ways, nevertheless that old story was enough to ruin Reb Zalmen's new career.

Reb Zalmen himself couldn't for the life of him understand why nothing came of the matches he proposed. Yet one time, when he became more insistent and started pestering the families to whom he'd proposed matches, he heard the mischievous little boys from a wealthy family calling after him, "Reb Zalmen, did the bride tell you she was pretty and shake your hand on it? Reb Zalmen, did the father-in-law promise he'd pay the dowry and shake on it?" Only then did Reb Zalmen remember the real handshake, and he understood why his matchmaking went nowhere. Reb Zalmen took it as punishment for not carrying out his mission for Reb Avrem Borekh.

And when Reb Zalmen returned to the shtibl, he put the fancy cane somewhere in a corner and decided to give up matchmaking. At that very moment his lust for money disappeared as well, and his mood lifted. He went to the wash basin, and poured plenty of water over his hands, as if purifying himself after a funeral. Reb Zalmen buried his nightmare about piles of money. And even though Reb Zalmen remained penniless for the rest of his days, the joy of a fervent Hasid never left him.

CHAPTER NINE

Reb Zalmen's Worldly Pleasure

1.

Reb Zalmen's face grew thinner. And not only his face, but his entire body. When he stripped in the mikveh, everyone saw that he was nothing but skin and bone, dried up like last year's *esrog*.

People in the Aleksander shtibl became upset seeing his thin, shriveled body. They would anxiously ask him: "Zalmen, are you feeling alright? Zalmen, perhaps you're not 100%?"

Reb Zalmen hated to hear people talking about him. He drew away from them, saying "I don't know what you're talking about!"

But they insisted: "Pretty soon there won't be anything left of you. Something must be wrong. Maybe you should go see Doctor Laypuner?"

"Leave me alone," Reb Zalmen thundered. "Why are you bothering me all of a sudden? The more flesh the more worms."

Still, it was obvious that Reb Zalmen could barely drag himself along, and he was growing weaker by the day. Little Itshele Kubats, who loved to tease Reb Zalmen, became more and more worried about his health. Without consulting anyone, he brought the healer Krakovski to the shtibl.

Krakovski, a tall man with a round, clean-shaven face, with large hands and feet and large grey eyes, gave the short and shriveled Reb Zalmen a sharp glance. He checked Reb Zalmen's pulse and announced, "This man must eat."

When Itshele Kubats asked the healer to write a prescription, the healer answered, "He doesn't need a prescription. The best medicine for this man is good food."

It had been a difficult, hot summer. There weren't many people in the Aleksander shtibl over the summer. Anyone who could get away went to their summer homes with their families. Only the poor stayed behind. Rarely did anyone offer a meal in the shtibl, and Reb Zalmen had almost nothing to eat—a piece of bread here, a cucumber, an onion. Rarely did he get any cooked food. By the end of the summer there wasn't much left but a bundle of bones.

We went to the country house that summer as well, and Reb Zalmen didn't even have a place to eat on Shabbos. It was the summer after the incident with the fish tail at Reb Shmuel's house, and Reb Zalmen absolutely refused to eat at anyone's house other than ours.

My father had arranged for him to go eat at the home of a wealthy Hasid, who kept a generous table and just happened to be staying in town this summer. But Reb Zalmen wouldn't even consider it. People argued with him: "Zalmen! What are you talking about? It's Shabbos! How can you pass up a Shabbos meal? Zalmen, you're insulting Shabbos!"

To that Reb Zalmen answered: "The Talmud says, 'Make your Shabbos like a weekday, as long as you don't have to beg from others.'" It seems that Reb Zalmen considered himself at home with us, but going to eat at a stranger's table was a different matter.

With all that, Reb Zalmen became weaker and weaker, but so gradually that he himself didn't notice. But when people came back before the High Holy Days and saw what had become of him, they realized that something had to be done quickly.

First of all, they raised a little money for Reb Zalmen. My father smiled as he handed the money over and said, "Zalmen, no doubt you remember the passage in Tractate Pesachim, commenting on the words: 'And all of the possessions at their feet' (Deut. 11:6). 'Rabbi Eliezer says, "This is a man's money, which sets him on his feet."' Here, take the money, and it will get you straightened out."

But everyone was astounded when Reb Zalmen refused to touch the money. The same Reb Zalmen who was always delighted when somebody handed him a coin didn't even want to look at the money now.

Reb Shloyme the gabbai sat down next to Reb Zalmen and reminded him of the story about the son of the Baal Shem Tov and Reb Pinkhes Koretser. Once the Baal Shem Tov's son came to see Reb Pinkhes in Korets. The Koretser Rebbe saw that he was depressed. The first thing Reb Pinkhes did was travel around the area and raise a substantial sum of money. When the Baal Shem Tov's son took the money, his depression disappeared, and he returned to his former spiritual level.

But no matter how weak Reb Zalmen was, he never got depressed. On the contrary, he was happy. The cheerful look on his bony face was so strange that it terrified people who saw him. Reb Zalmen's smile suggested that he understood everything, he knew everything, he had made his peace with everything ...

It was just after the time when Reb Zalmen had despaired of becoming a shadkhn, just after he had lost his passion for money. He felt liberated, like someone who's falsely accused and is suddenly released from prison.

People insisted Reb Zalmen take the money, but he wouldn't hear a further word about it.

At that point little Ithsele Kubats decided that he would feed Reb Zalmen. He took the money and began cooking for Reb Zalmen and serving him the food. He brought him two eggs for breakfast and bought butter and cheese. For lunch now and then he brought some broth with a bit of meat, and he made sure that Reb Zalmen ate dinner.

Reb Zalmen, who enjoyed eating but hated dealing with cooking and preparing food, was delighted that everything was brought to him ready to eat. What he enjoyed most of all was the broth with meat at lunch. He would have eaten the same thing three times a day, and he liked it hot and with plenty of fat.

Reb Zalmen gradually grew stronger. The odd smile that had frightened everyone disappeared from his face. In its place could be seen his usual cross expression. He regained self-confidence. His face began to fill out again. The first part to fill out was the tip of his broad nose, which he used to blow violently. Reb Zalmen started wanting specific foods. Suddenly he said to Itshele Kubats: "Today I want cutlets." And when Itshele brought the cutlets, he asked "And where's the broth?" He didn't want to hear that cutlets don't make broth. "I want broth with cutlets," he shouted.

Itshele Kubats wasn't rich himself, and he had seven children. He couldn't spend all his time cooking and serving Reb Zalmen. So they began to think about how Reb Zalmen could earn a modest, steady income and hire someone to cook for him.

2.

Since the winter term was just about to start, everyone figured that Reb Zalmen should think about taking on a few students. They thought he could tutor four or five boys from wealthy homes.

There were enough men in the shtibl who were prepared to have Reb Zalmen teach their sons. Even though they knew that Reb Zalmen was a stickler and "a stickler shouldn't be a teacher," nevertheless they liked his intellectual intensity. Together with his anger, Reb Zalmen often came up with a sharp saying that deeply impressed everyone who heard it. It was enough to make them enjoy his anger as well. The youngsters in the shtibl would deliberately start arguments with Reb Zalmen. Even though they knew he was right, they would annoy him with nonsensical questions. Then pearls would come forth from Reb Zalmen's mouth. The older Reb Zalmen grew the more he enjoyed a strong shot of liquor. So too, the older he grew, even though his voice became weaker and his enunciation worse, the more he enjoyed coming up with a sharp saying.

The boys whose fathers were planning to have Reb Zalmen teach them were eleven or twelve years old, good lads, who knew how to prepare a Talmudic text with the commentary of Tosafos on their own. All Reb Zalmen had to do was listen to them recite and then review with them the passage they had all prepared. For that, Reb Zalmen would be well paid for the time he could in principle have spent on something else, since he wasn't supposed to take money for teaching Torah.

The boys' fathers figured that Reb Zalmen would sharpen their minds. They hoped that their sons would be a good audience for his wit. Moreover Reb Zalmen liked to see people learning with intensity, diligently, with all their heart and soul. "Words of Torah will only be retained by someone who kills himself for them," Reb Zalmen would shout, stamping his feet as he repeated the quote from Tractate Berachot. He couldn't stand to see a student doing nothing, even for a minute. When he saw a boy who had come into the shtibl to review a passage getting lost in thought, or resting with his hands behind his head, or yawning, Reb Zalmen would really let the boy have it. He would slip behind the boy, grab a plump bit of flesh and give it such a pinch that the boy would almost faint from pain.

Plenty of fathers wanted Reb Zalmen to be their son's teacher. But all the plans foundered on the fact that Reb Zalmen didn't want to be a teacher. He wouldn't hear of it. Reb Zalmen, who enjoyed learning so much, didn't like teaching others. His view was that everyone has to do it on his own. But how can anyone know how to learn if no one teaches him? That wasn't Reb Zalmen's problem to solve!

Reb Zalmen bore a grudge against the Angel of Forgetting. It's well known that before a Jew enters the world, he's taught all of Torah. But at the moment when he's about to enter the world, an angel comes, strikes him above his mouth, and he forgets everything he's learned. That story infuriated Reb Zalmen. "And tell me why a Jew shouldn't be born a scholar? Isn't it enough that a Jew has to struggle on account of all the other demands in life, but he has to worry and fret over learning as well? Let the Goyim run themselves ragged trying to learn, since they don't have anything else to worry about. But a Jew has to know everything right away!" he would shout.

Reb Zalmen detested ignorant Jews. He persecuted them. Even little boys who hadn't studied yet he called "donkey heads."

When the boys would say to him, "Reb Zalmen, how often did your rebbe hit you because you were having trouble learning," Reb Zalmen was beside himself with anger. "What? Hit me? It wasn't because I couldn't learn that they hit me. It was because donkey-heads like you couldn't learn that I got hit!"

When a boy in the shtibl would start to feel comfortable enough to ask Reb Zalmen a question about a passage in the Talmud, he would shout: "Go away! What's wrong with you, can't you figure it out yourself?" The terrified boy would go hide somewhere in a corner.

People would try to convince him he should be more patient, saying, "Zalmen, don't you remember the passage in Tractate Rosh Hashanah: 'One who studies and does not teach, to what is he compared? To a myrtle in the desert, where no one can smell it.'"

But even that didn't change Reb Zalmen's mind: "Even if I knew that I was fated to be transformed into a myrtle in the desert, I'd prefer that to trying to teach these donkey-heads."

Some people thought that Reb Zalmen's unwillingness to teach anyone, even to translate a word or clarify a small point, came from the fact that Reb Zalmen himself was so focused. Everything that he had learned he had earned with the force of his own diligence, with his extraordinary desire to know. They assumed that was the source of his anger at everyone who came to ask him a question. Instead of working on it themselves as he had, they want the answer handed to them on a silver platter. The Angel of Forgetting had indeed made Reb Zalmen forget everything he had known before he entered the world, and he had worked for years to become a scholar—so everyone else should have to as well.

But when Itshele Kubats gradually stopped cooking for Reb Zalmen and taking care of him, and especially when Itshele began to skip bringing the broth, Reb Zalmen suddenly grew discouraged. He felt like a son-in-law whose support had suddenly been withdrawn. He remembered that winter was coming with its ice and snow. He imagined himself alone at night in the shtibl without a spoonful of warm food. Suddenly he felt sorry for himself. The bit of flesh he had been able to put on his bones since Itshele had begun to look after him aroused his sympathy, as one has sympathy for a newborn child.

Reb Zalmen became less self-certain. He walked around with his head bowed down. He began hesitantly approaching people. Eventually he let one of them know that he'd be willing to teach one or two boys.

But "Torah is acquired only in company," people insisted. One or two boys by themselves wouldn't learn much. Either Reb Zalmen had to take five boys, or he would get none. Reb Zalmen had no choice. A few days before the winter term began, during the intermediate days of Sukkos, at the very last minute he agreed to take on five boys. And that's how Reb Zalmen became a teacher.

3.

Reb Zalmen commenced his instruction. He taught them Tractate Shabbat. At first he did it altogether reluctantly, as if driven by some outside force. But gradually he melted and began to enjoy teaching. He derived malicious pleasure from the behavioral strictures that govern Shabbos. He became to imagine himself the sage Shammai the Elder, ruling all sorts of things forbidden on Shabbos. The things one is permitted, or at least not punished for, pained him. He was ready to condemn to stoning anyone who committed the least infraction of the Shabbos prohibitions, even inadvertently. Each of the thirty-nine primary categories of forbidden labor grew in his eyes into a mountain, just like Mt. Sinai, under which any Jew who dared to transgress might lie buried.

Reb Zalmen took all of the anger he felt at being forced into becoming a teacher and directed it at the subject of study. He taught the extra decrees meant to avoid explicit sins on Shabbos with such passion as if he had just declared them to be the law. He was ready to bind the Jews in iron chains to make sure they would always remember it was Shabbos and wouldn't think or breathe anything else.

After teaching one of these lessons, Reb Zalmen got up from the table exhausted. He would lie down on the bench for a while, until his broth came. The broth was brought by an old woman who had a room in a nearby house. After a long search Hersh Khayem the shammes had found this woman. She was a poor, childless widow. She agreed to cook lunch for Reb Zalmen every day. He wanted a fresh broth every day. For her labor, the woman got a platter of broth as well.

The first time she placed the bowl in front of Reb Zalmen, he turned up his nose. Somehow he didn't like it. He wanted a nice, yellow chicken broth, with big puddles of fat swimming around in it. The broth the woman gave him was pale and had almost no fat at all.

Reb Zalmen didn't eat long noodles, egg barley, or potatoes in his soup. He loved the broth itself so much that he preferred to sip it straight, without anything solid added. Just like he didn't like flavored spirits, he couldn't stand broth with anything other than fat floating in it.

The broths that Itshele Kubats used to bring Reb Zalmen came from rich kitchens, where they were made with chicken or turkey and some beef thrown in as well—so they were nice and fatty. But the widow made her broth out of just a bit of beef, so how could it be fatty?

But Reb Zalmen wasn't interested in excuses. A really good broth was his greatest worldly pleasure, and he wasn't about to renounce it on account of some poor widow. At first Reb Zalmen was ashamed to say anything about it. He sat there in a black study, nursing his resentment and growing angrier with every sip. Then he began to murmur something incomprehensible as he ate. The woman saw that he was displeased, and it dawned on her that it had something to do with the broth. At first she didn't dare ask him about it, but eventually she asked: "Reb Zalmen, is there something wrong with the soup?"

Reb Zalmen didn't look at the woman. He peered into the bowl and asked, "Really, this is supposed to be a broth?"

"What else could it be?"

"It's just water."

"Reb Zalmen, why do you say that? I put in a piece of beef and some chopped vegetables."

"A broth has to have some fat."

"How could I make it fatty? That little bit of beef and the vegetables don't have any fat."

"A broth without fat isn't a broth," declared Reb Zalmen, waving his hand as if to dismiss her.

Eventually Reb Zalmen began telling the boys that the woman was actually a thief. She kept the fatty broth for herself and gave him the thin, watery stuff. When he heard the woman coming he would say to the boys, "Listen, the thief is on her way!" He never referred to her other than as "the thief."

The woman learned from the boys that Reb Zalmen suspected her of theft. She wept and wailed. She threatened that her husband, who had been a scholar as well, would stand up for her and would know how to teach Reb Zalmen a lesson.

When she went out Reb Zalmen turned to the boys and said, "What's she crying for? A thief cries!"

It didn't make a difference. Reb Zalmen refused to accept that she wasn't cheating him.

The woman threatened to stop cooking for Reb Zalmen. Reb Zalmen threatened to stop paying her to cook. But he didn't have anyone else to cook for him and it was hard for her to renounce her daily plate of soup, no matter how skimpy it might be.

She took to bringing the entire pot of soup into the shtibl and showing everybody that she gave Reb Zalmen his portion first and only kept a bit for herself. But Reb Zalmen wasn't interested. "Don't you think I know that she took the fatty part for herself first?"

4.

During the winter the woman got sick and stopped cooking for Reb Zalmen. It was bitterly cold and he didn't have a bit of warm food. He would have been happy to get even a thin broth at that point. But the woman was quite ill and couldn't get out of bed.

Woe to Reb Zalmen! He had his habits: he ate at a certain time and then rested. And now this! True, the woman was a thief, but at least her cooking gave him a bit of energy.

What was he to do? One morning a student said, "Teacher, I know how to cook broth."

The boy's name was Moyshe. He came from a wealthy family who lived in the country. His father owned fields and forests in the region of Lublin. The boy had always lived in the country, but right at the beginning of the winter term his brother, who had gotten married and moved to Warsaw, had brought him to the city to study with Reb Zalmen.

At first Reb Zalmen wouldn't think of letting the boy cook for him. But the word "broth" was tempting. Reb Zalmen sensed a hole in his insides after a few days without broth at lunchtime. It was hard for him to concentrate. "I have no choice but to give up being a teacher," Reb Zalmen said out loud. But Reb Zalmen couldn't bring himself to make a boy waste study time cooking.

After an hour or so going back and forth, Reb Zalmen turned to the boy: "Listen, Moyshe, if you're telling me you know how to cook a broth, let's see what you can do. But do the cooking at your own home, not at that woman's place."

Reb Zalmen gave the boy some money. Moyshe went to see the woman to find out where she bought the meat. Then he went to the butcher, and then back to the woman's home. She had him bring next to her bed water, a pot, a ladle, and salt, along with the salting board. When everything was right next to her, she told Moyshe to come in half an hour, when she would have the meat washed, soaked, salted, and rinsed.

Half an hour later Moyshe came back. He took the piece of meat, a pot, and a kerosene stove and went to the shtibl. He put in the put a peeled onion, a carrot and some celery, along with the meat.

Moyshe interrupted his study from time to time to check on the broth. The last time he slipped out of the shtibl, he went into the nearby pharmacy, and bought a few pennies' worth of castor oil.

When Reb Zalmen went to rest after teaching, Moyshe went up to him and said, "Teacher, go wash your hands." He poured out a large bowl of broth, in which was floating a large spoonful of castor oil.

He brought the dish to the table, very proud of himself. As soon as Reb Zalmen looked at the bowl, he shouted triumphantly: "Ha! You see what that thief did! I knew she was cheating me all along! I knew she was eating the fatty broth and leaving me nothing but water!"

Reb Zalmen washed and recited the blessing afterward with profound concentration. Then he recited the blessing over a crust of bread and began to eat the broth. He was so pleased with the fat that he didn't even notice that somehow the taste was different.

But just about a quarter hour after finishing the broth, Reb Zalmen's insides began to churn. The castor oil on top of the hot broth upset him so much he thought he was about to die. Eventually he fainted and didn't even feel the pain in his intestines ...

The boy was terrified and raised the alarm. Neighbors came running. They put hot compresses on Reb Zalmen's stomach and tried various medicines, whatever they happened to have in the house. Reb Zalmen writhed in agony, dripping with sweat, and the diarrhea didn't stop …

It took a few days before Reb Zalmen really began to recover. And when he could stand up on his own again, he began to interrogate the boy who had fed him the broth. The shammes Hersh Khayem and Itshele Kubats were both present as well. First of all Reb Zalmen's bony hands delivered two fiery slaps to the boy's round, country cheeks. As soon as he felt the slaps, the boy confessed about the castor oil. He said that he wanted his teacher to have a nice fatty broth at least once.

Hersh Khayem and Itshele Kubats laid the boy down on the table and pulled down his trousers and underpants. Reb Zalmen took the boy's belt and began to lash him. He whipped the boy furiously as hard as he could. The boy screamed, but Reb Zalmen couldn't get enough. Suddenly he let go the belt, fell on the boy and bit his naked buttock …

Reb Zalmen fell away from the boy exhausted. Moyshe wailed as if witnessing the destruction of the Temple. Reb Zalmen shouted, "Listen, if I had killed you I would still be acquitted. Quiet! Don't cry, you'll be all better by the time you're ready to get married." And with that Reb Zalmen, who wasn't used to comforting anyone, awkwardly and roughly caressed the boy's tear-stained cheeks.

When he prayed that evening Reb Zalmen, who generally detested women, thought of the poor widow who cooked him his thin broths as he recited the passage "Heal us." When she got better, she began cooking his lunch again.

But Reb Zalmen wasn't interested in broth anymore. Now she brought him cooked cereal every day. As long as Reb Zalmen thought that he was spending enough for a fatty broth but the woman was cheating him, he insisted on broth. And perhaps he thought that she would eventually repent? But when it became clear as day that she really hadn't been cheating him and a little bit of meat really could only produce a thin broth, he didn't want it any more.

He also decided that he didn't want to continue teaching. On Purim he went to see the boys' fathers and told them they needed to find a different teacher for their sons.

Once again people argued with Reb Zalmen that he needed to make a living. But nothing helped. It didn't bother him at all that he didn't know where his next meal was coming from, that he didn't have a penny to his name. Once again he was contrary. He didn't want to study with anyone, didn't want to explain anything or answer any questions.

Reb Zalmen went to be with the Aleksander Rebbe for Passover. He was utterly cheerful throughout the whole holiday. When he handed the Rebbe a note with his request at the end of the holiday, all he asked for was health and fear of Heaven. He didn't even hint at money.

The Rebbe knew that Reb Zalmen had resigned from his teaching post. He read the note slowly and carefully. Then, from under the wide brim of his plush hat, he gave Reb Zalmen a sharp look and called out: "Zalmen, all is in the hands of Heaven except for the fear of Heaven. May you receive bodily sustenance."

As soon as Reb Zalmen left the Rebbe's room the Hasidim who had been with him during the encounter called out enthusiastically: "Zalmen, you'll be lucky now! Zalmen, buy a lottery ticket! You'll win—you'll see!"

But Reb Zalmen didn't want money anymore. He couldn't even think about it. He couldn't understand why the Rebbe had specifically mentioned material wellbeing, but he didn't try to figure it out.

That day they raffled off a set of the Babylonian Talmud at the Aleksander court. The income from the raffle tickets went to support the yeshiva boys. Reb Zalmen entered the lottery and won the Talmud.

All of the Hasidim were convinced that Reb Zalmen had missed a wonderful opportunity. They were sure that if he had bought a lottery ticket, he would certainly have won 75,000 zlotys.

CHAPTER TEN

The Story of the Goose

Itshele Kubats insisted that Reb Zalmen had to accompany him to visit Reb Shloyme the gabbai, who had lately lost all his strength and was living in a summer house in Falenica.

"Zalmen, Shloyme the gabbai explicitly told me that for God's sake, you have to go visit him," Itshele Kubats said to Reb Zalmen late one day after the afternoon prayers.

Reb Zalmen didn't approve of the summer colonies. He considered them a place of levity and licentiousness, where nothing of value was accomplished. And "let anyone who values his soul keep his distance." Any decent person had to stay miles away, and a Hasidic Jew—even more so.

When he happened to hear any of the Hasidim saying that they needed to get out of town in the summer for "fresh air," he would laugh bitterly. "There's no better air than in the Hasidic shtiblekh, and I feel sorry for anyone who can't breathe properly there," Reb Zalmen would mock the members of the congregation who spoke in tones of pious intensity about the fresh air of Falenica and Otwock.

"Ha, your wives, your wives want to go there," Reb Zalmen would tease the Hasidim in the shtibl as they were getting ready to head out for the summer. He winked at them with his narrow, red-rimmed eyes, as if letting them know he well understood that their wives were the bosses, and his face twisted in a disgusted grimace.

Reb Avrem Borekh, the rich man who was always in poor health, sat in the shtibl one evening, boasting to the paupers about the aroma of the pine forests at Otwock.

"You complete idiot," called out Reb Zalmen angrily, "one whiff of Darman's tobacco is worth more than all the aromas of all the trees in all of Otwock."

When the congregation began to disperse and head off to their summer houses, Reb Zalmen seethed with resentment. It simply infuriated him. Although he didn't really like socializing, he did like it when the shtibl was full. When the shtibl was crowded, when you couldn't move without bumping into someone, Reb Zalmen felt somehow different, better, safer. Even though he had his complaints against everyone and there was always some tension, he was glad to be interacting with a lot of people, reassured that there were people available for him to complain about. He liked to move around the shtibl from one room to another, muttering and grumbling loud enough for everyone to hear that he, Zalmen, was quite unimpressed by them.

Itshele Kubats reminded Reb Zalmen several times that they needed to go visit the ailing Shloyme the gabbai, but Reb Zalmen somehow always managed to put it off. Eventually Itshele Kubats wouldn't take no for an answer: "Zalmen, you should know that I told Shloyme the gabbai that we're coming to visit tomorrow. I'm coming too. I'll come pick you up, and I'll pay the fare both ways. I also ordered some really nice refreshments when we get there."

To this day I don't quite understand why Itshele Kubats was so intent on getting Reb Zalmen to go visit Reb Shloyme the gabbai in Falenica. Perhaps he wanted to show Reb Zalmen that the summer houses weren't such a bad thing after all. Or perhaps little Itshele, who loved to torment Reb Zalmen and say that Reb Zalmen wasn't really such a pious Jew—maybe he wanted to show Reb Zalmen the summer colony and get him to stop being quite so strict? Who knows what tricks the little Jew Itshele had in mind?

Be that as it may, this time Reb Zalmen couldn't come up with an excuse, and he gave in: "Okay, fine, I'll go."

The next day was a Wednesday. Right after the morning prayers and a bit of breakfast, Itshele Kubats came into the shtibl and called to Reb Zalmen: "Well, Zalmen, are you ready?"

"It's not such a big deal. It doesn't take much to get ready," Reb Zalmen answered contemptuously. He placed his cloth hat on his satin yarmulke, picked up his satchel which was by now more green than black, kissed the big mezuzah at the door, and followed Itshele out.

Itshele explained the itinerary to Reb Zalmen: "We'll take the local railroad rather than the main line, and we'll take the electric tram to the train station."

They went to Muranow Square, where Tramway #4, the one that went to Praga, was standing.

Next to the tram stood a little wooden booth. Tramway employees, motormen and conductors, sat nearby on benches. Each one of them had a piece of white paper opened on his lap, holding pieces of bread and ham or lard. The Christians washed down their lunch with milk or tea in bottles they carried in the side pockets of their dark-grey uniforms.

Reb Zalmen rarely left the shtibl. He had spent years inside it almost constantly. Only on Shabbos and on holidays, when he would come to eat at our house, would he walk a short distance away. And even then, the streets would be full of Jews on their way out from the shtiblekh, synagogues and study houses, carrying their tallis bags under their arms. They walked freely on the sidewalks. You wouldn't see a single Gentile.

When Itshele Kubats and Reb Zalmen arrived at Muranow Square and passed by the benches where the tramway employees were sitting so that they could get to the tram, the Gentile smell of pork assailed their noses. Reb Zalmen grimaced. The whole idea of this trip seemed wrong to him. He thought to himself: "Maybe I can turn around?" But Itshele was already standing on the tram's platform, tugging at Reb Zalmen to help him climb the steep stairs of the tram.

When they passed through Nalewki, Franciszkanska, and Swietojerska (which pious Jews called Yurske) Streets, almost everyone in the tram was Jewish. But when they reached Krasinski Square, Christians of various sizes and descriptions poured inside: big and tall, others thin, with smiling, open, round faces and with craggy, bitter and dour ones. They were all clean-shaven, and almost all of them had thick blond or grey-blond mustaches. They all carried briefcases, but some of them also had folded their black legal robes over their briefcases. Some of them wore black jackets and stiff black hats on their heads, and some wore black uniforms with green trim on their outfits and on their flat, round, black caps.

Older and younger Gentile women also got into the tram, carrying briefcases as well. They wore flat straw hats with navy blue or brown bands and light coats, gray or brown.

All of these people were lawyers and their assistants, notaries, bailiffs, and other employees of the courts. They were heading out from the courts, from the registry of mortgages, from the offices of the judicial secretaries, notaries and bailiffs, from the entire judicial apparatus at Krasinski Square, on Miodowa and on the nearby Hipoteczna. Some of these people were continuing conversations they'd begun in the courtroom. Others were just greeting each other. More and more frequently the tram passed by buildings upon which crucifixes were hung, and the Christian women crossed themselves while the Christian men doffed their hats. Suddenly the tram stopped short to let pass a slow funeral procession of priests and nuns, carrying crucifixes and lanterns. The Christian women bowed deeply and quickly crossed themselves. The Christian men stood up partway and took off their hats. Everyone stared, hostile and suspicious, at the two infidels, Reb Zalmen with his gray-white beard and disheveled sidelocks, and Itshele with his red beard.

Reb Zalmen twisted this way and that in his seat. The Gentile men and women, the crucifixes, the priests, all repulsed him. In his heart he cursed little Itshele for convincing him to undertake the journey. He balled up his firsts, trying with all his might to restrain himself from letting Itshele have it right then and there.

Little red-bearded Itshele sat across from Reb Zalmen, piercing him with glances from eyes alert, round, and brownish-pink like a squirrel's. He saw that Reb Zalmen was twisted with anger, but it gave him pleasure to see Reb Zalmen suffering, and he made no effort to hide from Reb Zalmen his malicious smile.

Itshele Kubats had the sense that Reb Zalmen didn't know what it meant to suffer the yoke of exile. Itshele himself had a terribly hard time earning a living for his family of nine, buying remainders from the Christian tailors. More than once he'd had to put up with insults from the Christian journeymen tailors, more than once he'd had to ignore things he'd never expected to put up with. More than once he'd had to smile at the filth that came out of the apprentices' mouths precisely when he was there to hear it. More than once he'd had to humble himself in order to earn his meager living, something as hard to achieve as crossing the Red Sea.

But Reb Zalmen stayed in the shtibl. A free bird, free of the yoke of exile. Years on end with no one except Hasidim. When he did go outside, it was only into the Jewish streets, and even then only with Jews from the shtibl.

So Itshele enjoyed seeing Zalmen tasting the bitter cup of exile. More than once during an argument he had shouted: "Zalmen! You've got it easy. Let me send you to see my Gentiles, and then you'll see what it means to be in exile."

Now little Itshele finally had a chance to take his revenge. He laughed right in Zalmen's face just when Reb Zalmen was most furious.

When the tram stopped on the other side of the Kierbedz Bridge, Itshele stood up, tugged at Reb Zalmen's sleeve, and winked to let him know he should follow.

As soon as they got off the tram and onto the sidewalk, a Gentile ran up to them and shouted at Reb Zalmen: "Hey, Jew, *peysi, peysi*," and pantomimed tearing off Reb Zalmen's sidelocks.

Reb Zalmen wasn't angry at the Gentile, because "it's well known that Esau hates Jacob." He was only angry at Itshele

Kubats, who had dragged him out of the shtibl and into the Gentile world.

Reb Zalmen was so angry he couldn't even stammer a word. He descended the stone steps leading down from the Kierbedz Bridge to the local train. There were many steps and they were steep. Reb Zalmen had no choice but to hold onto Itshele's arm, even though he couldn't stand him.

Only once they had gotten into the local train did Reb Zalmen take a deep breath. There was almost no one other than the two Jews in the long, narrow rail car. Reb Zalmen sat and closed his eyes to avoid seeing Itshele, and he gradually started to feel calmer and more relaxed.

But a few minutes before the train set off, crowds of Gentile women began streaming in, young and old, each one with a basket or a jug in their hands. They all wore red kerchiefs with flower prints, their blouses unbuttoned, their petticoats ample, and barefoot. Soon the car was so crowded that all of the entrances and all the spaces between the benches were occupied by these women, joking and shouting at each other. A young Gentile woman leaned against Reb Zalmen, trying to make room for her friend. Another woman standing nearby leaned her packages on his lap. Reb Zalmen made himself as small as possible, and drew in his hands and feet, trying to hide inside his coat like a tortoise in its shell, but the crowd of women pressed ever tighter against him. Reb Zalmen was totally at a loss. If he could reach Itshele now, he'd tear him limb from to limb. But the women had separated them, and the two Jews couldn't even see each other.

Little Itshele Kubats knew exactly what Reb Zalmen was going through. He kept smiling with pleasure. But he was careful to look in another direction, lest the Gentile women think that he was smiling at them …

At Anin Station, all of the Gentile women suddenly poured back out of the car. Reb Zalmen gave Itshele a look as though he were ready to swallow him whole. But Reb Zalmen was so relieved to be rid of the women that he didn't say anything at all to Itshele.

2.

When they reached Falenica, Reb Zalmen opened his eyes wide. Even at the station, everyone was Jewish. Heavyset coachmen with bronzed faces and thick beards, wearing Jewish hats and long caftans, stood carrying whips, waiting for customers to settle into the seats of their carriages, riding on large springs. Jews wearing dark coats and large cloth hats and women with their heads wrapped in black shawls dragged heavy sacks. Little boys with curled sidelocks in octagonal caps and long coats helped carry packages. People ran around, talked, shouted, and sweated. Right next to the station there was a marketplace. Jewish women stood in groups, wearing bonnets, long wigs, or kerchiefs on their heads, guarding baskets of fruit, vegetables, baked goods, eggs, butter and cheese, poultry live and slaughtered, shouting, calling, talking at the top of their lungs. Next to some of them stood men, thin, quiet as if ashamed, doing what they could to help their wives.

Reb Zalmen suddenly found himself in a world of Jews. He felt at home. His soul warmed up. At least he could stand to look at little Itshele now, but he still couldn't say a word to him.

They crossed the marketplace and entered a street lined with villas on both sides. The villas were surrounded by picket fences, half-collapsed, half-rotten with time and rain. Around the villas walked Jews, in pairs or solo, with high velvet yarmulkes on their head, dressed in blue calico nightshirts, beneath which wide, long fringed undergarments peeked out. They chatted amongst themselves or walked alone, lost in thought. Jews with pale, yellowed faces lay on lounge chairs, reading small-format religious books that they held in their thin hands. Other Jews sat at tables on their verandas, studying out loud. At some of the villas several boys sat underneath a tree with an older man, enthusiastically studying. The sound of Torah could be heard at nearly every house.

Reb Zalmen, who had always loudly proclaimed that the summer colonies were full of levity and licentiousness, was quite astonished to see and hear all this. Next to him went Itshele Kubats, who enjoyed Reb Zalmen's bewilderment. Little Itshele knew that not far away there were places called Miedzeszyn, Michalin, and Swider where males and females bathed together half-naked, may we be preserved! But Itshele didn't say anything about that to Reb Zalmen, and allowed himself to bask in Reb Zalmen's confusion.

Reb Zalmen and Itshele arrived at the villa where Reb Shloyme the gabbai was staying. It was a small, low-roofed bungalow the color of a dried-out mushroom. The veranda was supported by a few beams with little piles of wood dust at their feet. On it was a wooden armchair, and on the armchair was a rubber pad, and on that sat Reb Shloyme the gabbai, underweight, with a yellowed face.

Reb Shloyme was delighted to see his guests. He greeted them with a warm "Sholem-aleykhem!" and ordered chairs to be brought for them, so they wouldn't have to sit on the plain benches that lined both sides of the long table. Reb Shloyme's wife served tea. Reb Zalmen asked her to add more of the tea concentrate, since he loved strong tea. He stirred in several chunks of sugar and smoked a cigarette.

"Zalmen, why are you smoking cigarettes? It's a shame, you're spoiling the good air here," said Reb Shloyme.

"Up till now I thought that these summer colonies were just levity and license, and now I realize that I was being silly," Reb Zalmen cheerfully admitted.

Reb Shloyme couldn't believe it: "Zalmen, don't you feel it? Can't you sense how good the air is here?"

But Reb Zalmen had a damaged throat and a nose full of smoke from the various brands of cigarettes he constantly cadged from others. He drew a deep breath through his nose, but couldn't smell anything except cigarette smoke. He didn't answer Reb Shloyme, but just looked at him with a contemptuous smile, as though Reb Shloyme were kidding himself or had been deceived by others ...

They drank a few more glasses of tea. They sipped slowly, sighed and chatted. Then Reb Shloyme proposed that they take a tour of the house before lunch.

But Reb Zalmen didn't want to budge. "We don't have to, it's fine here," Reb Zalmen replied. He had no intention of giving up the spot where he was sitting. Somehow the interior of the summer house still made him nervous. Out on the veranda he felt at home, and he didn't want to take any risks.

The lunch was a generous one, with spirits, salted snacks, an appetizer and a nice, fatty broth, the kind that Reb Zalmen loved. Then there was a platter of meat, and stewed fruit to top it off.

Reb Zalmen ate with a hearty appetite and enjoyed everything. He just didn't understand why it was necessary to travel to the country to enjoy all this, when it was available in Warsaw. But he didn't say anything further.

As evening drew near little Itshele said to Reb Zalmen, "Well, we'd better get ready for the trip back." Reb Zalmen wasn't eager to go, but little Itshele urged him on.

Before they finished their goodbyes Reb Shloyme's wife came out to the veranda carrying a substantial package wrapped up in paper and said: "Reb Zalmen, here's a properly slaughtered goose. Here it costs four zloty, but in Warsaw any housewife will be happy to buy it for seven. Also, the goose is already plucked, and it'll be a bargain for a Warsaw housewife."

Reb Zalmen shrank back in distaste. "Please forgive me, but I don't want to carry a goose around."

"Reb Zalmen, you won't have to carry it around. At the first fine home you come to, they'll give you seven zlotys and be grateful for it. You'll earn a few zlotys, and when you get a chance you'll pay me back the money."

Reb Zalmen impatiently shrugged his shoulders, as if to say, leave me alone!

Itshele Kubats spoke up: "Reb Shloyme's wife, put the package on the bench, I'll take it. Everything will work out."

Reb Shloyme's wife put the package on the bench. Itshele picked it up and placed it under his arm. They took their leave,

Reb Zalmen saying, "Shloyme, enough of this foolishness with the summer house. Come back to Warsaw already."

3.

They took the regular train back to Warsaw. Night had fallen, and the semi-dark railroad car was almost empty. A few worried Jews sat silently, from time to time tugging at their beards with gestures of desperation.

Reb Zalmen dozed almost the entire way back. The two men walked back to the shtibl from the Nadwislanska Station. Itshele Kubats carried the package. When they reached the gate of the building where the Aleksander shtibl was located, Itshele slyly managed to slip the package with the goose into Reb Zalmen's hands and disappeared.

Reb Zalmen stood there, not knowing what to do. The nerve of that Itshele! Reb Zalmen had been sure that if Itshele took the goose, he would deal with selling it. Once again he began to resent the entire idea of going to visit Reb Shloyme at the summer house. Reb Zalmen was sure that nothing good could come of it. If he met up with that good-for-nothing Itshele Kubats now, he'd put an end to him for sure. Reb Zalmen didn't know what to do with the package, but he couldn't bring himself to just throw it away.

The next morning Reb Zalmen realized he had no choice but to take the goose and go sell it. But at every Hasidic home to which Reb Zalmen went to try to sell the goose, they didn't want to buy it because they didn't trust a slaughterer they didn't know, and on the other hand Reb Zalmen didn't want to go to any of the houses where they wouldn't be so careful about the kosher slaughter. He couldn't lower himself that far.

In Warsaw at that time, many of the religious households weren't quite so insistent on avoiding meat that had been slaughtered by someone they didn't know. Times were still good in Poland then, including for the Jews, and there was plenty of poultry for the Jews of Warsaw. The slaughterers in Warsaw had more than enough, and they weren't worried if some slaughtered poultry was brought in from the countryside.

The very homes to which Reb Zalmen brought the goose were precisely the ones where they were still careful to use only locally slaughtered meat. Reb Zalmen thought that people would trust him and wouldn't have any qualms. If Reb Zalmen said it was kosher, then certainly at least the Radziminer or the Kalebyeler Rebbe should be willing to eat it!

"What's the problem? If I'm bringing it to you, you shouldn't hesitate," Reb Zalmen argued with the housewives.

"Reb Zalmen you are, but we don't eat any meat except from our own slaughterers, and that's it," the women answered.

Reb Zalmen spent a few hours going from door to door like this, and the goose became heavier and heavier. He passionately cursed Itshele Kubats. The paper in which the goose was wrapped became worn and torn. The white-pinkish flesh of the plucked goose peaked out here and there, and Reb Zalmen's discomfort kept on growing. He was embarrassed by the naked goose and its round thighs. It was more than he could stand.

Reb Shloyme's wife thought that Reb Zalmen would find the easiest place to sell the goose and go straight there. But Reb Zalmen wasn't the sort to look for the easiest place. He wasn't about to sell the goose to just anyone.

Reb Zalmen spent nearly a whole day trying to sell the goose, without success. He was beyond despair. All he could think about was finding Itshele Kubats and tearing into him.

Reb Zalmen was exhausted. It was a hot day. The wrapping paper was completely tattered. Reb Zalmen was reduced to carrying the goose by its neck. From a distance it looked like a little Jew was carrying a giant goose which was cut into slices, the slices hanging to the ground.

While Reb Zalmen walked along in despair, a young man approached and stopped him. The young man pointed to the goose and asked, "Mister, are you selling it?"

Reb Zalmen took the young man's measure with a hostile look. He saw someone who was cleanshaven and bareheaded, but with a fine, noble, Jewish face. Reb Zalmen hesitated: Should he deign to sell the goose to this person? He couldn't make up his mind.

"Mister, what's taking you so long? If you want to sell it, fine—and if not, not."

Reb Zalmen was ready to get rid of the goose once and for all. He nodded yes; he was ready to sell.

The young man looked over the goose as if he were an expert. He lifted it up to inspect it, and squeezed its breast a few times. "Mister, how much do you want for the goose?" he asked.

"Seven zloty."

"You'll take six. It's not such a great find. There are so many geese you could pave the streets with them."

Reb Zalmen reached out his hand, ready to take the goose back. "Mister, hold your horses. If you weren't a religious Jew, I wouldn't dream of paying you seven zloty."

Reb Zalmen was silent. The young man rewrapped the goose in the strips of torn paper and placed it under his arm. He took a wallet out of his breast pocket and handed Reb Zalmen a twenty-zloty note.

"I don't have any change," said Reb Zalmen.

"Mister, take the twenty zlotys and go into a store where you can break the twenty. I'll wait here. I'm not worried-you're not going to run away with my twenty."

Reb Zalmen took the note and went into a nearby grocery store. He waited for a customer to finish, and then asked the storekeeper: "Change this twenty for me."

The storekeeper took the paper note, lifted it up, placed it under a lamp, looked sharply at Reb Zalmen and asked, "Mister, where did you get this twenty?"

"What?"

"It's counterfeit."

Reb Zalmen's face grew pale. His heart began to pound. He grabbed the twenty and ran out into the street. But there was no trace left of the young man or the goose ...

Toward evening, by the time for afternoon prayers everyone in the shtibl knew the story about the goose.

The little Jew with the red beard, Itshele Kubats, went on the offensive. Before Reb Zalmen could tear into him, he attacked: "Zalmen, you're so arrogant that you don't even know how to take advantage of an opportunity. You don't even have a drop of humility in you. And if you're not humble, you're not a Hasid. Your kind of Hasidism is just pretense. Not only aren't you a Hasid, you're not much of a Jew at all. If you weren't so arrogant, you could have sold the goose first thing in the morning, and no one else would have given you any trouble."

Reb Zalmen listened to every word, and just this once, he didn't try to answer Itshele right away. He just gave him a look dripping with such contempt that not just one little Jew like Itshele could have been annihilated, but ten such Itsheles. Then Reb Zalmen spoke up quietly, as if to himself, "If there is no decency there is no Torah, and if there is no Torah there is no decency."

Reb Zalmen wasn't at all troubled by the fact that he'd been swindled out of the goose with counterfeit money. What bothered him was that he'd lowered himself, been willing to forego the honor due Torah, the honor due a Hasid, and stood there in the street ready to do a deal with just anyone.

But Reb Zalmen held the summer colony to be the main culprit. True, he thought to himself, the summer colony may not be a place full of levity and licentiousness, but it always has its ways to drag a person down from the straight path ...

CHAPTER ELEVEN

The Billy Goat's Yortsayt

In the town of Aleksander, close to the city of Lodz, a billy goat was born.

What difference does it make where a goat is born? But this one, born on a winter night in Aleksander at the home of a poor Jew, on a bundle of straw in a dank kitchen, was a special kind of goat.

It wasn't special because it was born in the town where a famous rebbe lived, where he kept his court and where thousands of Hasidim from the four corners of Poland would gather for the High Holidays. No, there were plenty such towns in Poland, towns where rebbes lived, where they kept their courts, and where thousands of Hasidim used to gather for Shabbos and holidays. But the goat this story is about was different from all other goats.

The goat born in Aleksander that winter night at the home of a poor Jew was a firstborn, the sanctified fruit of its mother's womb. But in addition to being a firstborn, evidently either it was a reincarnation of a Hasid or it had something of a Hasidic soul.

As soon as the goat was able to walk, it was irresistibly drawn to the Rebbe's court. When the goat wanted to scratch itself—and that was quite often—it would run even from the other side of town to scratch itself against the fence of the Rebbe's courtyard. It couldn't scratch itself anywhere else.

This particular goat wouldn't think of eating regular goat food. He only wanted food cooked in the Rebbe's kitchen. The goat could get by all week long with a piece of the Shabbos challah or some cold Shabbos kugel, as long as it came from the Rebbe's kitchen. He only ate as much as was necessary to keep body and soul together.

When his beard began to grow, somehow it wasn't a regular goat's beard. The hairs weren't the straight, simple hair that a goat grows. It was simultaneously soft and strong, multi-stranded and silken.

In the goat's bright, pale pink eyes glowed the purity of the great blue sky. Endless goodness and patience radiated from them. You could see that the goat was ready to take on itself all the burdens of the world, that it was ready to sacrifice itself as the goat sent to Azalzel, if the world so demanded.

The goat's long face with its protruding chin somehow resembled a kabbalist who had spent many years tormenting his body. Somehow the goat seemed to bear the secrets of a hidden world bound up in its mute mouth. He had the serenity of one who knows everything, for whom everything is clear. It seemed as though the goat somehow was able to cut through the confused reckonings of this world and come up with a simple grand total.

The goat's horns twisted back in on themselves. They looked like two handles turned on a lathe so one could grasp them, like holding on to the horns of the holy Altar in times of danger, when one's mortal fate is about to be decided.

The goat was thin. Its forehead was wrinkled, like an old man's. Thick brows grew over and around its eyes, and it looked like the goat wore a pair of heavy eyeglasses. Its pelt was yellow and black, like the colors of a Turkish tallis. Occasionally the goat would hide among the thin trees in the Rebbe's courtyard, and it looked as though a small, thin Jew stood wrapped in a tallis in solitary meditation.

And that's how the goat looked as it wandered through God's world, with its thin legs like stalks of flax. It always seemed deep in thought, as if lost in the supernal realm, always ready humbly to help carry anyone's burden.

Since the goat was a firstborn, dedicated to the Temple, they couldn't slaughter it unless and until it developed some kind of blemish. But no matter how skinny and weak the goat was, it never developed the least blemish. Somehow it seemed that could never happen to this goat.

And even if the goat did develop a blemish, who would have dared to slaughter something that had the face of a kabbalist? No one. Not even a heartless slaughterer would have dared to do it. It would be different of course if the Rebbe would have explicitly said it was time for the Hasidic soul reincarnated in the goat to be redeemed.

But for now, the Rebbe didn't even hint at such a step.

Again, because it was a firstborn, the goat could not be made to work. It wasn't even needed as a stud, because as Rashi comments on the verse "two hundred nanny goats and twenty billy goats": "Two hundred nanny goats only need twenty billy goats, and so it is with all male animals." A ratio of one to ten, that is, and it so happened that in Aleksander there were already two males for ten females.

Moreover, it was clear that the goat was a celibate. If it saw a female in the distance, it would turn away and tremble in fear just like a Hasid who suddenly imagines a naked woman, may we be preserved!

The goat spent entire days wandering around the Rebbe's court like a lost soul. From time to time the Rebbe's grandchildren would jump up on the goat's thin back and ride for a bit. Naturally, they only did that when no adult was looking. But gradually riding on the goat's back became their chief pastime. The goat willingly bent down to let the holy kids get on its back.

Our Reb Zalmen was a close associate of the goat. Even though Reb Zalmen loved to eat and rarely got enough for himself, he would share anything he had with the goat, and he didn't feel like he was losing out. Reb Zalmen also made sure that neither the Rebbe's grandchildren nor any random Hasid got on the goat's back. More than once Reb Zalmen went to the Rebbe to tell on the grandkids if they rode on the goat anyway.

The Hasidim around the court were astonished by Reb Zalmen's friendship with the goat. He didn't like animals, and he didn't even bother looking at them, and he didn't like people either—not Hasidim and certainly not Misnagdim, who were his mortal enemies. Or better: he liked Hasidim in the abstract, but not as individual flesh and blood.

So why did he like the goat so much? Some Hasidim hinted that evidently Reb Zalmen knew something that even *He* (that is the Rebbe) didn't know. Some asserted that Reb Zalmen was a contrarian, and this was contrarian behavior. If everybody thought he was a misanthropic sourpuss, he would show them the opposite. And maybe it was just the other way around, and he wanted to emphasize his hostility to humans: "You I dislike, but I love the goat dearly." Whatever the reason, the minimum of love for fellow Jews that every Hasid must show was channeled into Reb Zalmen's love of the goat.

But it never occurred to anyone that the goat might one day repay Reb Zalmen for his kindness.

In the course of time this very special goat came to seem quite ordinary. Not only did the Rebbe's grandchildren shamelessly ride the goat, but even wise guys who weren't related, rich sons-in-law of Hasidim, took a ride. Even older Hasidim would take a turn after a few drinks. The goat would open its naïve eyes or knit its brow in puzzlement, like a young student struggling over a commentary of the *Maharsha*. And more and often the goat would bend its back under the weight of anyone who wanted to ride, as if it were clear as day that this was its fate.

Until one day—and later on, no one quite remembered what day it was—the crowd gathered at the Rebbe's court got so wild that they didn't give the goat a moment's rest as they took turns riding it. As soon as one got off the next got on.

The goat didn't resist. It carried the Hasidim on its thin weak back all day, and it was as if one could see reflected in its eyes the words, "For to this you were born ..."

But late in the afternoon, when the crowd gathered to recite the afternoon prayers, the goat made its way into the southwest corner of the yard, extended its hooves, raised its head to Heaven, sighed deeply and released its mortal soul.

Following the rules concerning such a firstborn, the skinners weren't allowed to take its hide. It was buried in a little field not far from the Rebbe's courtyard. When the body of the goat was lowered into the pit, it looked like a Jewish corpse wrapped in a tallis.

2.

Reb Zalmen always enjoyed a little festive meal at the shtibl, even more than the other regulars. It wasn't that he thought those festive meals were such an essential part of being a Hasid. Nor was it that he desired to be part of a "band of brothers together." No, that wasn't the reason.

As you know, Reb Zalmen didn't like people. He complained about everybody. He complained about the rich and even more about the poor. He complained about religious people and even more about those who didn't bother being religious. He didn't like anybody.

He didn't like the rich because he considered every rich person guilty of something until proven innocent. He was ready to believe the worst of every rich man, whether or not he was a Hasid. Itshele Kubats said that Zalmen's hostility to the rich was really a display of envy, because Zalmen himself knew that if he had money there were all sorts of things he might do. Even my father, at whose table Reb Zalmen ate for years, Reb Zalmen somehow disliked, and would never pass up a chance to try to teach him a lesson.

Reb Zalmen disliked paupers because he was one. And the hostility of one pauper to another is even greater than his hostility to the rich.

He disliked pious people because they convince themselves that shouting out their prayers, clapping their hands enthusiastically, praying endlessly, in short everything that's just external display made them close associates of God. Reb Zalmen couldn't stand that.

From time to time a Lubavitcher Hasid who lived nearby would stop into the Aleksander shtibl. When the Lubavitcher would go outside to use the outhouse, he would come back in, pour massive amounts of water over his hands, pick up the hand towel and carefully dry his hands while holding them upright, and recite out loud the blessing afterwards. He emphasized especially the words "Who has created in us various hollows and various openings."

Reb Zalmen really couldn't contain himself. He would rush up to the Lubavitcher with his hands balled into fists and shout, "Listen, you Lubavitcher, you really think that every time you go outside to pee everybody in the shtibl has to hear about it?"

And the ones who weren't so pious, all of whom Reb Zalmen dismissed as frivolous, he disliked because they make their lives too easy. He used to say, "A Jew can't make things easy on himself. Everything should be difficult. Being Jewish is like crossing the Red Sea. You earn it with the sweat of your brow. You have to stand on your head in order to gain a bit of real Jewishness."

What irritated Reb Zalmen more than anything were the Hasidim who left the city for the summer with their families. On Shabbos in the summer, when the shtibl was half empty, Reb Zalmen sat there and stewed. "It's one thing for the rich Jews or their wives to go to the spas. A rich person can do what he wants. But everyday Hasidim who barely manage to get by, what are they doing in the country all summer long? Who knows what kind of things go on there?"

When people came back from their summer homes, Reb Zalmen let everyone hear him say: "Oh, the people who can't be bothered with Jewishness showed up. They're afraid to show up for the Day of Judgment at their summer homes."

Reb Zalmen disliked Hasidim because they convinced themselves that putting on a shtreimel and going to see the Rebbe now and then made them Hasidim. Being a Hasid means suffusing oneself in Hasidism like being soaked in a mikveh. "You've got to lower yourself into Hasidism until it's over your head." Reb Zalmen pointed to the crowd: "But they take it a spoonful at a time, like medicine, when you're really sick."

And Misnagdim he disliked even though he held that there was nothing there. He considered their Jewishness empty and dry like a stalk of grain stripped by the wind. Sometimes Reb Zalmen actually felt sorry for the Misnagdim, whose Jewishness was like a body without a soul. But when he was angry he dismissed them with a wave of his hand as people who took God's bountiful world and ruined it.

And that's why, even though Reb Zalmen liked a little community meal, it wasn't because he got to eat together with everyone. Reb Zalmen liked those meals because he was hungry. Any weekday when a crowd happened to gather at the shtibl Reb Zalmen would pace back and forth among them anxiously. He wanted to sense somehow, maybe with his sense of smell, whether there would be a feast. And often enough there was. People took advantage of any occasion to set out some food for everyone.

Really elaborate meals, with fish and meat, were held on the yortsayts of the deceased Aleksander or Vurke rebbes. But when even an ordinary Hasid had yortsayt after his mother or father, it wasn't enough for him to offer a shot of brandy and some cookies, he had to make it at least a modest meal. If he didn't have enough money of his own, the congregation took up a collection, sent someone out shopping, and made a meal of it.

And a siyum, celebrating the completion of study of a holy text absolutely demanded a feast. Every Rosh Chodesh called for a festive meal. If there was a dry spell without a yortsayt or a siyum, they would focus on someone who had been sick, even with just a cold. They'd convince him he'd been dangerously ill, and now that he was better, he was obligated to offer a thanksgiving meal. He might protest that it was nothing, he hadn't even gone to the doctor—it didn't help. Itshele Kubats had a trick to make the fellow so afraid that he'd think he really was dangerously ill and had no choice but to provide the meal when he got better. And again—if the person who'd been ill didn't have money, they'd take up a collection. The point wasn't the money; it was having some reason for a meal together for the sake of the mitzvah, rather than just for the food itself.

Such meals usually took place in the evening. You could see Reb Zalmen's divided self then. Good and bad, amiability and anger, touchiness and calm, all reigned inside him at once. Now he was bad and then suddenly good—relaxed and chatty. Now he was approachable and suddenly he became furious again.

But all the same it was clear that Reb Zalmen thoroughly enjoyed the meal. Even Itshele Kubats would offer him another piece of herring, a hard-boiled egg, or another glass of beer, and enjoyed seeing Reb Zalmen's pleasure.

3.

One frosty winter night, there were only a few people in the shtibl. Here someone was studying, there a couple of others were discussing Hasidism. The oven in the middle room gave off plenty of heat, and it was pleasantly warm there. Folks sat drinking hot tea with chips of sugar between their teeth. In that cold weather most people stayed home rather than coming to the shtibl. On the other hand, those inside didn't want to go out onto the alien, frozen street.

Reb Zalmen sat near the stove drinking tea. Someone called out, "You know, on a night like this it would be really nice to have a meal, especially with a bowl of hot groats."

Reb Zalmen lifted his head. In his red-rimmed eyes burned a yellowish fire. He looked at the speaker with a piercing, demanding glance.

"It's not a bad idea at all," was heard from a corner.

"Who? What? When?" inquired an elderly Jew who sat next to the table, innocently taking snuff.

Reb Zalmen gave the old man such a dirty look that the man didn't dare open his mouth for the rest of the evening.

Reb Zalmen was silent. His wrinkled brow grew even more creased, like a badly rolled ball of yarn. You could see that he desperately wanted there to be a meal. Whether it was because he was hungry or because he didn't want to be left alone on a cold winter night, Reb Zalmen became a different person. His arrogance disappeared among the wrinkles of his parchment face. He was so humble that it was heartbreaking to see.

Even Itshele Kubats responded, "Yes, we really should have some kind of meal." And when Itshele Kubats said yes, no one was going to say no.

But there had to be a reason. No one was going to come to a Hasidic shtibl and organize a meal just to fill their bellies. So people started casting around for a reason. No one in the shtibl had yortsayt, no one was completing a course of study, none of them had recovered because none of them had been ill. It wasn't the yortsayt of a rebbe, either.

Someone picked up a calendar showing the yortsayts of all of the Hasidic luminaries. At first they looked for the yortsayt of a rebbe connected with the Kotsk tradition, then someone connected to Rizhin, then Lubavitch, and finally those who had left fewer followers.

But as luck would have it, not a single Hasidic rebbe had died that day. Should they resort to celebrating the yortsayt of a great Misnagid? Or maybe even see if it was the yortsayt of one of the rebbes of Ger, strange as it would seem to celebrate that in an Aleksander shtibl ... It nearly came to that, Heaven forfend.

The situation was dire. People were ready to give up on the idea of a meal. Reb Zalmen sat gloomy and discouraged.

In time someone noticed that Reb Zalmen's yellowish face looked different. His creased, shrunken face swelled red. He started breathing heavily, as if something were choking him. Suddenly he stood up and shouted, "Jews!"

"Zalmen! Zalmen! What happened? What's with you?"

Reb Zalmen leaned on the white tiled stove, as if he were afraid of falling. He covered his eyes with his hands as if trying to rid himself of a disgusting bug that wouldn't go away. He drew a deep breath, opened and closed his mouth a few times and then shouted again, "Jews! Do you know whose yortsayt it is today?"

"Tell us, Zalmen! Tell us, let's hear!"

Reb Zalmen trembled. He seemed bewildered, like someone who has to do a terrible deed and can't bring himself to do it. Then he called out: "Jews! Today is the goat's yortsayt!"

The crowd wavered, stood there astonished, didn't know what to do. But it only took a few sentences until people reached into their pockets. Everyone shook out whatever he had, and they raised a fair bit of money.

They brought in a pot of groats stewed with calf's bones from Itshe's restaurant. They also brought a roast goose, brandy, beer, bread and rolls. It was a royal feast. They hadn't seen a meal like that in the Aleksander shtibl in quite some time.

That wasn't the only time they celebrated the goat's yortsayt with a festive meal. Any time the people in the Aleksander shtibl wanted to have a Hasidic meal and couldn't find the right occasion, they would call out that it was the goat's yortsayt, and they would have a great time eating, drinking, and discussing Hasidism.

The yortsayt of that goat, the firstborn, the one with the face of a kabbalist, with a bit of a Hasidic soul, or perhaps the very transmigration of a Hasid, was celebrated several times each year in the Aleksander shtibl.

Reb Zalmen had the place of honor at every such meal. His face was animated, and his mood was cheerful, and his tongue was loosed. They never heard Hasidic stories from Reb Zalmen's mouth like the ones he told on the goat's yortsayt.

And thus it became clear to everyone why the sourpuss Reb Zalmen had been so drawn to the goat, why he had shared his last bit of food with the goat …

The goat repaid Reb Zalmen many times over. All of the Aleksander Hasidim said that if the goat had come into the world only so that Hasidim would be able to sit together, eat, drink, and enjoy their meal—that itself would be a lasting merit, and its death—even more so.

CHAPTER TWELVE

Midrash Rabbah

Of all the texts that one might study, much as Reb Zalmen enjoyed digging into the more difficult discourses in the Talmud or the complex commentaries by the Tosafists or the Maharsha, his greatest pleasure was studying the compilation known as *Midrash Rabbah*.

It wasn't the parables, the commentaries, or the legends contained in that book that he liked. No. He enjoyed the Biblical verses brought together in the midrash from distant places in the Hebrew Bible. For example, when he opened up Midrash Rabbah to the section on the Book of Numbers and reviewed the first few words: "'And God spoke to Moses at Mt. Sinai' as the verse says (in Psalm 36), 'Your judgments are like the great abyss,'" Reb Zalmen's shrunken face filled out and a discrete smile hovered around his lined mouth. The further the second verse from the one it was supposed to illuminate, the greater the logical distance between them, the closer the link between them in Reb Zalmen's eyes. He reacted to them like someone who sees an intimate friend who has unexpectedly arrived from far away.

Reb Zalmen believed that one can only understand what is incomprehensible. One can only grasp the ungraspable. Only what's distant from everyday reason is a real source of insight. For the truth is that it's not you who can grasp anything with your own reason; rather reason seizes you, it takes you prisoner. But whatever you cannot grasp cannot grasp you, either. That makes you a free person, which in turn allows you to grow in wisdom.

That's what Reb Zalmen was like when he was in a good mood, but for him, being in a good mood didn't mean relaxing. He never relaxed. Being in a good mood for him meant merely that he was ready to make peace with the world against which he constantly struggled.

When Reb Zalmen was angry, when he wasn't getting along with himself and certainly not with the world, he turned to such difficult studies. Sheer intelligence was everything to him then. And his intelligence was bitter and sarcastic. He never sought to lift another up with his sharp wit, but rather to bring the other lower; not to give pleasure but to give pain. When he realized that people nevertheless enjoyed his wit, he sensed that they had deceived him, that they had somehow cheated him into giving them something he had never intended to give.

Since Reb Zalmen appreciated precisely that aspect of the midrash that was most scholarly and arcane, he resented the fact that simple folk were taught Midrash Rabbah and *Eyn Yankev*.

"Women and unlearned men should only be taught the Shulchan Aruch, each one according to his practical needs. The women need to be taught which commandments they are obligated to observe, and which sins they must not commit. It's the same with the ignorant men. They have to know what they're allowed to do and what's forbidden. That's what they have to be taught, and nothing else!"

Reb Zalmen had no patience for women studying the Yiddish Bible adaptation, *Tsene Urene*. One autumn Shabbos afternoon he sat at our table, sipping tea and waiting for the third meal. Suddenly he heard coming from the next room the voice of my great-aunt Beyle, who lived with us just then, reading that volume out loud. "*And the human was created*," she read in a slow, intense voice: "On the sixth day God said to the angels, 'Let us make a human.' Thus God teaches us that a person shouldn't be arrogant, rather he should consult with others when he wants to do something. Even if they are of lower status, he should ask them. And also God asked the angels because a person has a face like an angel. The angels would envy humans, and that's why God consulted with them first ..."

That was enough for Reb Zalmen. He was beside himself listening to the familiar tones in which my aunt narrated God's speech to the angels. Reb Zalmen ran to the door of the room where the women were sitting and shouted: "Listen, Mr. Jewish Lady! Better get the meal ready! It's not your business whether God consulted with the angels or not."

Reb Zalmen didn't even know who was reading Tsene Urene—my aunt, a stranger, or even my mother. It didn't matter. He couldn't contain himself.

My Aunt Beyle, whose husband deeply respected her, looked at our insolent guest as if some plague had suddenly appeared. But my mother, who was already well acquainted with Reb Zalmen's brazen behavior, smiled and winked to my aunt as if to say, "Keep reading, don't pay any attention to him."

Reb Zalmen was furious at the preachers in Warsaw who used to address the simple crowds in the synagogues and study houses. He couldn't stand the Lithuanian style preachers who used to threaten everyone with the fires of Gehennom for the least transgression. But he had even less patience for the Polish preachers who promised Paradise for those who fulfilled commandments, and who retold and explained the legends and midrashim as if they were simple stories.

Reb Zalmen held that all of these texts were esoteric, and the Talmud says: "Six things are said of an ignoramus, and one of them is that it is forbidden to reveal secrets to him." That was said in reference to an everyday secret, so what are we to say about the Torah, which is entirely esoteric? As the *Zohar* says: "There is not a single word or letter in the Torah that does not contain extraordinary secrets." So how can the preachers come and turn those secrets into stories for women and ignorant men, Reb Zalmen seethed.

Nevertheless, when Reb Zalmen was in a good mood, he liked to study Midrash Rabbah on his own. He swam the seas that seemed to separate the cited verses, buoyed up by legends, commentaries on the legends, and parables, with everything that he believed only true scholars knew, but that must be kept far away from women and ignorant men.

The passage in Midrash Rabbah that Reb Zalmen most enjoyed studying was in the section on the Torah portion Ki Tisa, in the Book of Exodus.

2.

When Reb Zalmen first appeared at the Aleksander shtibl in Warsaw, which was then still on Nalewki Street, Hersh Khayem was the shammes. When Hersh Khayem was arranging things in the shtibl, filling the kerosene lamps, straightening the long benches, Reb Zalmen told him what to do. When Hersh Khayem opened the Ark of the Torah to look for a scroll that was already rolled to the portion to be read on Shabbos, Reb Zalmen stood near the open Ark and pointed to the scroll that Hersh Khayem should take: "This one, not that one!"

At first Hersh Khayem looked at the newcomer as if he wasn't quite right in the head. But when he saw that Reb Zalmen was making himself at home in the shtibl and becoming more self-confident and stubborn by the day, Hersh Khayem became afraid of Reb Zalmen. He realized that Reb Zalmen was very much in his right mind. He feared that Reb Zalmen might gradually start to interfere in Hersh Khayem's affairs and might want to steal his position altogether.

Hersh Khayem began to distance himself from Reb Zalmen. Not only wasn't he interested in Reb Zalmen's opinions, but even when Reb Zalmen wanted to help him move the heavy benches, Hersh Khayem drove him away. He stopped in the middle of moving the benches and grumbled: "Listen, Zalmen, who's the shammes here, you or me?" And he wouldn't move the benches any further until Reb Zalmen let go.

Hersh Khayem began to torment Reb Zalmen. He spread rumors and did everything he could to get Reb Zalmen out of the shtibl.

This was right after the death of the second Aleksander Rebbe, the author of the Yismekh Yisroel. Some of the Aleksander Hasidim broke off and started following the Biala Rebbe, Reb Aren. Reb Zalmen agitated in favor of Aleksander and against Biala. He sang as loudly as he could, so everyone in the shtibl might hear:

"Let's all stay together,

"Let's go to Aleksander."

That didn't keep Hersh Khayem from telling the most devoted Aleksander Hasidim that Zalmen was a hypocrite, that he might be shouting "Aleksander" but his heart was for Biala.

The regulars at the Aleksander shtibl divided into pro-Zalmen and anti-Zalmen camps. The most patriotic Aleksander Hasidim believed that Reb Zalmen had to be immediately and completely banned from the shtibl. Their opponents were equally firm in support of him. They believed that no Jew should be banned from the shtibl. My father was with the latter. They didn't see any evidence that Reb Zalmen was leaning toward Biala.

And Reb Zalmen himself wasn't easily swayed. He was old enough to have traveled to be with the old Rebbe, the Rabbi of Pilts, the Rebbe Reb Yekhiel. He wasn't about to be dismissed so easily. He shouted at Hersh Khayem: "Listen you! I can chew up your kind to chase a shot of liquor! What do you think you are?"

It was at that time, in fact, that Reb Zalmen settled permanently in the shtibl. The very struggle to exclude him established his right to be there. The Aleksander shtibl was his home until the end of his days.

Actually Reb Zalmen never dreamed of stealing Hersh Khayem's meager living. Reb Zalmen had no intention of running the shtibl. He knew it wasn't for him. He was an expert in one thing: Reb Zalmen. He knew that he was stubborn, didn't get along well with people and certainly couldn't serve them, because he couldn't stand to be subservient to anyone, not the secretary of the shtibl and not its richest member.

Reb Zalmen had no possessions of his own. The shirt on his back and his daily bread were donations, and so was every penny in his pocket. But Reb Zalmen had opinions about everything.

He wasn't only sure of his opinions in matters of scholarship or Jewish law, not only when it came to Hasidism. He wasn't merely the spokesman in every dispute among Hasidim or between adherents of different shtiblekh. He stuck his nose into everything, always said what he thought, never wanted to retreat, arguing instead that he was right and things must be done his way.

It was curious that Reb Zalmen, who had nothing, wanted to be a partner in everything. If two Hasidim had words with each other, it was Reb Zalmen's affair. If there was an argument between Aleksander and Biala Hasidim, it was his business. If there was a fight in the shtibl against the worthless Hasidim who had the nerve to come inside wearing cloth caps, the commander in chief was Reb Zalmen. When it came to deciding who would be called to the Torah, Reb Zalmen expressed his opinion. He felt he had to be in charge when money was collected on Purim, or for Passover food for the poor, or before Yom Kippur.

But Reb Zalmen didn't only consider himself a partner in the Aleksander shtibl's affairs, but also a partner in the running of God's world. Not only do humans have free will; Reb Zalmen believed further, along with Maimonides, that God had as it were handed over the running of the world to them.

3.

Time continued on its way. People forgot when Reb Zalmen had first appeared in the shtibl. He became part of the shtibl itself, and no one could imagine the place without him. He'd been our steady guest for some time, and we, too, had become used to his brazen ways.

One Saturday evening a group of Hasidim sat at our house waiting for the meal to see out Shabbos. It was late in the winter, before Purim, but the weather was dry and cold. Everyone was sitting in the big dining room, still warm from the big stove that had been heated before Shabbos. A meat borsht with bones and beef was boiling in the kitchen. There was fish and challah left over from Shabbos.

Meanwhile everyone sat at the table, drinking tea and smoking cigarettes. My father and Shloyme the gabbai smoked cigars.

Reb Zalmen had been at our place since lunchtime. After we ate he'd taken a nap on the big leather couch in the dining room. Before it grew dark he got up, recited the afternoon prayers and ate the third meal. Then he waited for *havdole*, and now he was sitting at one end of the table waiting for the Saturday night meal.

I was playing in the next room with my sisters, peeking into the dining room from time to time to see what was going on. I was about ten or eleven then. And one time when I went into the room, Reb Zalmen called me: "Khilish, come here."

None too eagerly I approached Reb Zalmen. He pulled over an empty chair and said, "Sit here, next to me, you've played with girls long enough."

That didn't please me at all, because I was in the middle of a game of fan tan with my sisters. Even though I was old enough to be studying Gemara with the commentary of the Tosafists and others, I was a spoiled only son among five girls, and I spent a lot of time playing with them.

But I had no choice except to sit down next to Reb Zalmen. He stood up, went to the bookcase and took down a huge volume of Midrash Rabbah. Then he sat down, opened the volume and said, "Well Khilish, we'll learn some midrash, okay?"

It was the Torah portion Ki Tisa. Reb Zalmen found the right part of the volume, but he didn't start at the beginning. Rather he went to the story about the Golden Calf. He recited the text intently as always. Suddenly I heard the words of the

Midrash: "And Rebbi Nekhemye said, 'At the time when the Jews did *that thing*, Moses stood up to appease God. He said, "Master of the World, they made you a helper and you are angry at them. This calf that they made can assist you. You make the sun rise and he will make the moon rise; you the stars and he the constellations; you make the dew fall and he will make the wind blow; you make the rain fall and he will grow the plants." And God replied, "Moses, you too are as mistaken as they. The calf is nothing."'"

Even though Reb Zalmen usually studied quickly and intently, when it came to Rebbi Nekhemye's words, he began to recite slowly and melodically, as if reciting the Song of the Sea during the morning prayers. He drew out every word as if it contained a hidden sweetness. He played with each word as if it were a precious jewel, and he didn't neglect to stab me in the back of the shoulder with his bony finger to make sure that I read out loud as well.

But I looked at Reb Zalmen more than I looked at the midrash. Somehow he seemed as cheerful as if he'd just had a big drink of liquor. I could tell that he enjoyed the words of the midrash immensely. But I couldn't tell where that pleasure came from.

When Reb Zalmen noticed that I was looking at him instead of at the book, he poked me in the shoulder again and began all over: "And Rebbi Nekhemye says …"

The people sitting around the dining room table wondered what was going on, what Reb Zalmen was studying with me. They knew Reb Zalmen very well, and they knew how much he hated teaching others or even explaining a detail. Evidently they assumed that I was somehow special.

And I was no less puzzled. Indeed, that was the first and only time that Reb Zalmen studied a text with me, although he did tell me Hasidic stories which I would repeat years later, when I was far from the tradition myself.

Among those waiting for the Saturday evening meal was Itshele Kubats. Along with his various responsibilities in the shtibl, he was something of a secret agent. He knew which of the young men slept late on Shabbos morning, which one read a secular newspaper, which one considered himself too sensitive to go into a cold mikvah on a winter Shabbos morning. He knew if a lad forgot his afternoon prayers. More than one such had gotten a beating from his father because Itshele told on him. Itshele also reported to the Rebbe himself the various misdeeds of the young men in the shtibl. At least, that's what people claimed. And the boys and young men were terrified of Itshele.

That Saturday evening Itshele sat with the crowd, smoking cigarettes and casually chatting with my father. But his left ear was paying attention to every word Reb Zalmen read with me.

Suddenly I sensed that I was being looked at. I raised my head from the volume and saw my father and Itshele staring at me, while Itshele was saying something very serious to my father.

At that moment my father called out: "Zalmen, leave the kid alone, let Khilish be. Let him go play, and you, Zalmen, come closer, sit next to me. I want to teach you how to smoke a cigar."

Reb Zalmen stopped reciting the text. He sat in confusion and maybe even in fear for a moment. He closed the book and stood up. I seized the moment and went to the other room to finish the game of fan tan with my sisters.

4.

Like a range of events and sayings that I heard in my childhood and that stayed in my memory even though I didn't understand them at the time, and later rose to consciousness from time to time modestly demanding an explanation, so too that winter Saturday evening and the strange way Reb Zalmen studied the midrash on Parsha Ki Tisa with me stuck in my memory.

Years passed. I was no longer observant, but on Shabbos and holidays I sat at my father's table. Occasionally I would study one of the holy books, and I still loved to discuss Hasidic lore with the Hasidim.

I maintained good relations with Itshele Kubats, whose red beard had by now turned partly gray, even though in my younger years his tattling to my father had cost me dearly. Our friendship was based on a common passion for the work known as the *Shney Lukhos Habris*. I loved the author's honesty and modesty, for writing "Know that 'loving your neighbor as yourself' will cause you to 'love your God.'" For years that was practically the essence of my worldview.

One Thursday evening Itshele Kubats sat at our home studying a volume. He was waiting for my father, who had just come home from work. I don't know why, but when I looked at Itshele I suddenly thought of Reb Zalmen and the midrash on the portion of Ki Tisa we had studied that winter night. I wanted to know more about Reb Zalmen. I thought that might help me understand what motivated him to study that passage with me.

But I was afraid to ask the "secret agent" Itshele Kubats about Reb Zalmen. I always had the feeling he could read my mind. I had the sense that you always had to approach him indirectly so he wouldn't guess right away what I had in mind. I began with a simple question:

"Reb Itshele, how is Reb Zalmen? I haven't seen him for at least a week."

"Your Reb Zalmen picks fights with everybody."

"Why 'my' Reb Zalmen?"

"I know you're his Hasid, you love his weird notions."

"How could I be his Hasid? I don't even know who he is or where he comes from."

I could tell I was getting warmer. I saw down on the couch next to Itshele and offered him a cigarette.

"He's from Shedlets, or so they say, but beyond that I can't say who he is."

"And when did he come to the shtibl, and why did he come to Warsaw in the first place?"

Little Itshele opened his round eyes wide, took my measure from head to toe, picked up the cigarette, took a deep drag and began to relate: "When Zalmen came into the Aleksander shtibl on Nalewki, none of the Hasidim knew what had brought him to Warsaw to be a guest at other people's tables and to live in the shtibl. He came without a penny in his pocket. I remember as if it were today that they had to raise money in the shtibl for his very first breakfast.

"At first people thought that Reb Zalmen had come to Warsaw for a few days. They wanted to give him money so he could sleep at an inn. But he didn't want it. He wanted to stay in the shtibl. He had brought with him a small pack that he never touched when anyone else was present.

"At that time I was still a young man, just past my wedding, but they already said that I was a wise guy," Itshele confessed. "I was very curious to know what Zalmen had in his pack. Once, when Zalmen left the shtibl for a few minutes, I quickly examined its contents. I saw a red blanket, a pillow, a desiccated satin coat, and a badly worn fur hat with only half its top left.

"That's when I understood that Zalmen had come to Warsaw for good, that the shtibl was to be his home.

"Reb Shloyme the gabbai and Hersh Khayem the shammes bitterly resisted. There was no way they wanted to let Zalmen live in the shtibl. In addition to the general principle that a shtibl can't be a hostel, they were afraid to have someone staying there unofficially. And they couldn't report that he was living there, because the lease explicitly stated that the shtibl was only a place to pray. People began to understand that Zalmen's sleeping in the shtibl was risky, because the janitor might report it to the registration officer, the officer to the landlord, and the landlord might get an order of eviction and throw everything in the shtibl out in the street.

"The registration officer had been watching the shtibl for quite some time and was looking for an excuse to be rid of it. He wasn't a Shabbos observer. He smoked cigarettes in public on Shabbos. The shtibl with its Hasidim, Shabbos and holidays, with its singing and dancing weren't to his liking. It irritated him no end.

"Hersh Khayem took the lead in the effort to make sure Reb Zalmen didn't stay in the shtibl. He was afraid that Zalmen might cause him to lose his job, because if the shtibl was closed Hersh Khayem would be left without a crust of bread.

"Whatever Reb Shloyme and Hersh Khayem did to try to get Zalmen out of the shtibl, it was no use. I remember as if it were today Zalmen shouting that a shtibl where a Hasid couldn't stay twenty-four hours a day isn't a Hasidic shtibl—it's a Misnagdic bag into which you can throw your tefillin."

"You know, Reb Itshele," I interrupted him, "the shtibl on Nalewki really did look like a bag full of holes. It was a narrow, long room with five windows that looked out on a blank wall."

"What are you imagining?" he retorted with a wave of his hand. "You knew the shtibl later, when the Shtrikever Hasidim pushed their way in. But before that there was nothing Misnagdic about it. Even though it was a long, dark room, it was cheerful and lively there. We had meals together, we danced and sang."

"And what became of Reb Zalmen?"

"Gradually people got used to the idea that he lived in the shtibl. Later, when Hersh Khayem began spreading the rumor that Zalmen was sympathetic to Biala, it didn't make any impression. Even your father, Khilish, who was so dead-set against Biala, didn't let them touch Zalmen. I don't know why, but somehow your father just took a shine to Zalmen.

"So gradually it came to seem as if Zalmen had a permanent right to live in the shtibl. They bribed the janitor so that he wouldn't tell the registration officer. Later, when the officer did find out about it and went to tell the landlord, the landlord told him to keep quiet. There was a lot of new housing in Warsaw at that time, and many apartments sat empty. One developer after another went bankrupt. It wasn't easy to find a tenant for that kind of space.

"But the main reason," continued Itshele, "the main reason why everyone got used to the idea that Zalmen lived at the shtibl was because they felt sorry for him. Even though nobody ever found out what had brought Zalmen to Warsaw, they all understood that he must have experienced some personal disaster. Something had happened to him or to someone in his family. When Zalmen came to Warsaw he was just beyond middle age, hardly an old man. So how could it be that a Jew that age never goes home, and instead he sleeps on a bench and lives on handouts? It's hard to figure out."

"So did anyone ever try to figure out what had happened?" I was dying to know.

"No, they didn't. Even though we knew he was from Shedlets and they called him Zalmen Shedletser, nobody investigated further. Do you know why? We were afraid we might turn up some really ugly information ... You know that I want to know everything. You remember how I got you to admit that you'd stopped saying your afternoon prayers, and I watched your father give you a good thrashing," Itshele winked at me, satisfied with himself. "But I didn't want to know about Zalmen. I was afraid to know ... You know that I'm a little suspicious of him. Sometimes he says things that you'd expect to hear from a great man's mouth, but it scares me when he says them. Those thoughts aren't for Zalmen. He's still a mystery to me. I've thought about him a lot. There's something fishy there. But why do you need to know all this? And—" but suddenly little Itshele realized that he'd already told me too much.

After my talk with Itshele I often thought about Reb Zalmen. More than once it seemed to me that I was beginning to understand the connection between Reb Zalmen and the bit of midrash he had studied with me. It became clear that this particular midrash fit Reb Zalmen's mood well. I began to understand that after Reb Zalmen's own world at home had collapsed, he might well take comfort to think of how the world must have trembled during the episode of the golden calf.

It seemed to me somehow that Reb Zalmen still felt the world trembling. It had never really recovered, never really found its bearings. And everything that happens in the world is miraculous, not the workings of nature. And in that world of the miraculous, somehow Reb Zalmen was able to sense a spark of personal redemption.

And perhaps—an even stranger thought occurred to me—perhaps that pauper Reb Zalmen, who never had enough for even the next meal but always had his own opinion, who wanted to have a say in how the world was run, perhaps he thought that in this world still shaken by the Jews' idolatry he might have some influence.

Whether it was what Moses said to God about the calf helping Him run the world, whether it was what happened to Reb Zalmen himself, or all of these things—a host of thoughts struggled with each other in Reb Zalmen's mind. But who knows what they were? Who can say anything for sure?

Years later, after Reb Zalmen had died, it was once again the little Itshele Kubats who brought us the news. I felt the urge to go to the shtibl, where I'd been absent for years, and where Reb Zalmen now lay dead. In the innermost room, next to the bench on which he had slept for years, he lay on the ground, covered by his threadbare satin caftan. Underneath the caftan one could barely see his earthly figure, small as the body of a ten year old. It was so quiet in the shtibl that it seemed that not only sounds, but even echoes had been banished. Next to the candles burning by Reb Zalmen's head lay his sack. The sack was almost empty; the only thing it contained were the worn-out remnants of what had once been his fur hat.

On the windowsill next to an empty chair lay a book. I picked it up: Midrash Rabbah. I wanted to look at the midrash. The book opened to a dog-eared page. I looked at the page: "And Rebbi Nekhemye said, 'At the time when the Jews did that thing ...'"

I smoothed the pages, undid the dog-ear, brought the book into the other room and placed it in the bookcase with all the other books.

CHAPTER THIRTEEN

The Inheritance

"Khilish," Reb Zalmen called me, "take this glass and tell Genendl to pour me another glass of tea but remember to tell her that first she has to put in the concentrated tea and then the hot water. You always have to remind her."

It was a summer Shabbos afternoon. Reb Zalmen woke up from a short nap on the wide leather sofa in the dining room. After his rest he sat at the table drinking glass after glass of tea. He sipped it slowly and loudly, and he sighed in pleasure.

I took the glass and saucer into the kitchen and said to the servant girl, "Genendl, pour Reb Zalmen another glass of tea, but remember to put in the concentrate and then the water."

"What? More tea? That man's already sipped half the hot water. Others will come, and there won't be any tea for them. I'm not giving Reb Zalmen any more tea."

"It's not your business how much Reb Zalmen drinks. Pour him the tea and bring it to him," I said in a quiet but authoritative tone.

Genendl's broad, pimpled face grew pale with fury. She looked at me, and then all the pores of her faces reddened. She took the glass, went to the jug, poured a glass of hot water and only then added a bit of concentrate.

She planned to bring the glass of tea into the dining room, but at the last minute she was afraid to go through with it. She went to the sink and poured out the tea. Then she picked up the bottle of concentrate, poured a bit into the glass and only then filled it with hot water. She brought Reb Zalmen a real kosher Shabbos glass of tea, placed it before him and said, “Drink it in good health, Reb Zalmen.”

Reb Zalmen pulled the glass close and looked at it. Then he took the heavy silver sugar bowl which stood on the table. He opened the sugar bowl, took the tongs out, and picked up with his fingers a few pieces of blue-white sugar, which he put in his tea. He took the silver teaspoon and held it in his hand for a second.

He took the first few sips with his spoon. Then he took it out of the glass, looked at the mark certifying that it was pure silver, put the spoon on the saucer and sipped the hot tea from the glass. Just as he liked to slowly sip the strong liquor, he loved to carefully sip hot tea or soup, and he never burned himself.

My father hadn't gotten up yet from his afternoon nap. I sat in a corner of the big leather sofa reading the Ethics of the Fathers, which my father studied with me on Shabbos afternoons in the summer.

The room was filled with Shabbos afternoon quiet, ripe and full as a tree in full leaf on a hot, windless summer day. Only Reb Zalmen's sighs of pleasure after every sip gave a hint of the material world in that mellow, ethereal Shabbos atmosphere.

On the dark brown oak credenza, decorated with mirrors and colored bits of crystal and plated with shining copper, stood a large bowl of crystal and silver full of fruits, reddish-green peaches and golden pears. The fruit was waiting for my father. After he got up from his nap and drank some tea, he would make a blessing and share the fruit with anyone who was in the house.

The sun, past its zenith, cast a broad swathe of light in the large, half-darkened dining room though the windows of the Venetian balcony on the side. The window was covered with a thick, cream-colored curtain.

The rays that made their way through the thick curtain fell to the side and lit the credenza. The rest of the room, whose walls were covered with heavy, dark brown wallpaper, remained half in shadow. Only at the credenza did the rays enter the prisms of the polished mirrors and pieces of crystal. Their golden light pierced the fruit in the crystal bowl and spread generously over the credenza's copper plating.

The table was also of dark oak. When fully opened it seated twenty-four people. Sixteen Hasidim comfortably sat there during a Shabbos kiddush. It had substantial feet carved into semi-circles, along which there was a fabric underhang. The feet were also covered with copper on the bottom.

Around the table stood twelve heavy, brown, high-backed chairs upholstered in leather. At the head of the table was an armchair with an even higher back.

Beyond the credenza stood the sofa. On either side of the sofa there were two bolsters, also covered with leather. Attached to the front of each of them was a copper lion with a ring in its mouth. I sat next to one bolster, closer to the credenza. In one hand I held the volume of Mishnah, and with the other I played with the ring in the lion's mouth.

Reb Zalmen raised his head from the glass of tea and looked around the room. He stared at the table covered with a snow-white cloth, which still bore the candelabra and the silver candlesticks. He looked at the credenza, at the brightly lit crystal bowl of fruit. He looked at the chairs, at the curtain, at the bronze gas lamp, at everything in the room. He seemed amazed, as if seeing all of this for the first time.

All at once his gaze rested on me. He seemed as if he'd just noticed me sitting in the corner of the sofa. With his red-rimmed eyes he took in once again everything in the room, and he turned to me and said, "Khilish, after 120 years this will all be yours," as he waved at everything in the room. "All this, and the business, and everything your father owns—it will all be yours and only yours. You shouldn't give the girls a penny, they'll be married already. According to Jewish law, they get nothing. You hear? NOTHING! Don't give them a thing. You're the only son, and you get everything."

As usual, Reb Zalmen spoke with passion. He looked at me and his eyes were full of envy. Perhaps it wasn't so much envy as pride, some kind of joy that all this would be mine.

Why Reb Zalmen should have taken pleasure in the fact that this would all be mine after my parents died, I couldn't say. Perhaps his deeply ingrained hostility to women made him glad that according to Jewish law I would get all of my father's estate and my sisters nothing. Whatever it was that made him happy, his very happiness made me lonely and fearful.

I can't claim that I wasn't proud to hear Reb Zalmen say that everything would be mine. His envious looks somehow made me feel important. For a second I felt like a big shot, but just for a second: the "after 120 years" made me feel so lost that Reb Zalmen's happiness made me want to cry.

I was about ten or twelve years old at that time. I'd often heard Hasidim say "until 120," "after 120." I understood that had something to do with life and death, but it never occurred to me that it might have something to do with my own father.

I gave Reb Zalmen a pained look. I wanted to get off the sofa and run away into the other room. But Reb Zalmen's red-rimmed eyes kept me glued to the spot with their strange joy, their angry illumination, and I was seized with fear.

It took a long time before Red Zalmen realized that far from being pleased that this would eventually be mine, it made me sad and depressed. He frowned as if biting on something sour. He looked at me contemptuously. Finally he waved his hand: "What's the point of talking to a kid who's still in short pants. Go join the girls!"

I left the volume of Ethics of the Fathers open, got off the sofa and ran away from the room where that strange Reb Zalmen sat.

Several years later, on various occasions, Reb Zalmen reminded me that everything my father possessed would eventually belong to me, and I shouldn't give anything to my sisters. He always said it with a kind of joyful envy and every time, even when I was wearing long pants, even when I was an adult, his words elicited sorrow and fear in me.

In my childhood I noticed and understood many things. But death was alien and impossible. As long as I could remember, no one had died in our home. My mother said that we had lost a small child, but that was before I entered the world. I had no personal acquaintance with death at that time.

In the Warsaw courtyards where we lived children and adults sometimes died. Sometimes I would see a black hearse enter the courtyard. But that had nothing to do with our family …

Later, much later, my grandmother died in ripe old age. But that wasn't in our home; she had lived with my uncle, her son, and I wasn't even at her funeral. Afterwards from time to time I would hear that an aunt, an uncle, a cousin or just an acquaintance had died. Eventually I personally encountered death and the dead. But I still retained my childish confidence that this all had nothing to do with my family.

Reb Zalmen died suddenly, the quick death that God grants to some. He took off his tallis and tefillin after praying, lay down on the bench, and his soul departed.

My father died much later. He managed to die in his own bed, in the first months of the terrible time of God's withdrawal from us.

All I have of my parents' estate is the bit of Jewishness which they planted in me, sometimes gently and sometimes harshly, carefully tending it and guarding it like their most precious possession.

These Jewish letters that I wrote now—they are what I inherited from my parents. They *are* my parents. Everything else they left behind is mixed with the smoke and dust of Jewish Warsaw.

My sisters are no longer. They died, and I cannot share my inheritance with them.

Perhaps those who share with me the feeling of being part of a Jewish family, perhaps they will accept from me, share with me what I've inherited from my Jewish home long ago …

May it be so. Who knows?

NOTES

Introduction

1 Marcin Wodziński, "Controversies Over Hasidic *Shtiblekh*," in his *Hasidism and Politics: The Kingdom of Poland, 1815–1864* (Portland, OR: The Littman Library of Jewish Civilization, 2013), 44–76.

2 David Biale, David Assaf, Benjamin Brown, Uriel Gellman, Samuel C. Heilman, Moshe Rosman, Gadi Sagiv, and Marcin Wodziński, *Hasidism: A New History* (Princeton, NJ: Princeton University Press, 2018), 537.

3 Marcin Wodziński, *Historical Atlas of Hasidism* (Princeton, NJ: Princeton University Press, 2018), 54.

4 Glenn Dynner, *The Light of Learning: Hasidism in Poland on the Eve of the Holocaust* (New York: Oxford University Press, 2023), 79.

5 Tzvi M. Rabinowicz, ed., *The Encyclopedia of Hasidism* (Northvale, NJ: Jason Aronson, 1996), s.v. "Warsaw."

6 By "denizen" is meant here more than someone who frequented the place. In this respect at least, Reb Zalmen would not have been unique: "Some particularly zealous Hasidim spent nearly all their time in the shtibl; for them it was like a home." Biale et al., *Hasidism*, 436.

7 Antony Polonsky, YIVO Encyclopedia of Jews in Eastern Europe, s.v. "Warsaw" at https://encyclopedia.yivo.org/article/487

8 Saidiya Hartman, "Venus in Two Acts." *Small Axe: A Journal of Caribbean Criticism*, Vol. 12, No. 2 (June 2008), 1–14.

9 See, for example, Aren Tsaytlin, "Der khoyze fun lublin," in his *Literarishe un filosofishe eseyen* (New York: Congress for Jewish Culture, 1980), 269–277 and "Der yid hakodosh," idem, 285–291. For a thumbnail sketch of the entire School of

Pshiskhe, see Elie Wiesel, *Souls on Fire: Portraits and Legends of Hasidic Masters* (New York: Random House, 1972), 203-207.

10 "Whether or not Pshiskhe was especially scholarly, rational, and antimystical, the primary image that later writers cultivated about this school was its practice of telling the unvarnished truth and its equally uncompromising rejection of social hierarchy." Biale et al., *Hasidism*, 338.

11 Dynner, *The Light of Learning*, 4.

12 See Biale et al., *Hasidism*, 354. Although the rivalry between Ger and Aleksander goes unmentioned in *Reb Zalmen*, as does Hasidic participation in Polish parliamentary politics, both were salient aspects of interwar Polish Hasidic life. Thus while the Gerer Rebbe and his Hasidim were prominent in the new Agudat Yisrael party, their efforts to enlist the Aleksander Rebbe and his Hasidim in the early 1920s were rebuffed. Gershon Bacon, *The Politics of Tradition: Agudat Yisrael in Poland, 1916–1939* (Jerusalem: Magnes Press, 1996), 193-4.

13 Morris M. Feierstein, "Aleksander Hasidic Dynasty," in YIVO Encyclopedia of Jewish Eastern Europe at https://encyclopedia.yivo.org/article/184, consulted August 10, 2025.

14 Generally on the turn toward inherited leadership, and the reasons why it came later in central Poland than elsewhere, see Glenn Dynner, *Men of Silk* (New York: Oxford University Press, 2006). Despite the death of the Rebbe and untold numbers of Aleksander Hasidim at the hands of Nazis and their accomplices, there is a community, albeit relatively small, of Aleksander Hasidim in the twenty-first century. Wodziński, *Historical Atlas of Hasidism*, 198.

15 That concern, to the extent it is historical, seems even more puzzling given the vast numerical superiority of Aleksander over Biale. In the first decades of the twentieth century, Aleksander was the second largest Hasidic group in Poland, with some 165 shtiblekh in various cities while Biale could boast only 18. Wodziński, *Historical Atlas of Hasidism*, 118. That volume is an astonishingly fruitful source for reimagining the Hasidic world.

16 Abraham Joshua Heschel's English-language portrait of the Kotsker, a substantially different text, is *A Passion for Truth* (New York: Farrar, Straus & Giroux, 1973).

17 Dynner, *The Light of Learning*, 6.

18 See Marcin Wodziński, *Hasidism: Key Questions* (New York: Oxford University Press, 2018), 265–268. For a different region (Galicia), my teacher Shlomo Noble related that after his father returned from serving in the Austrian army, he found that his *shtreiml* (fur hat) had been sold to buy bread—and it appears he never returned to wearing it. "In general, life grew less and less traditional all the time." Jonathan Boyarin, *A Storyteller's Worlds: The Education of Shlomo Noble in Europe and America* (New York: Holmes & Meir, 1994), 39, 63.

19 Dynner, *The Light of Learning*, 7.

20 Dynner, *Men of Silk*, describes this process of "professionalization" of Hasidism in Central Poland, albeit focusing on a somewhat earlier period. Reb Zalmen's opposition to this process was echoed by at least one decidedly historical figure in the same period. See Wojciech Toreck, "Mystic, Teacher, Troublemaker: Shimon Engel Horovits of Żelechòw and the Challenges of Hasidic Education in Interwar Poland," *Jewish Quarterly Review*, Vol. 110, No. 2 (Spring 2020), 313–342, especially 318.

21 "The journalist Tzvi Scharfstein considered the general educational disparities a recipe for disaster: 'The father is a complete Hasid, he educates his sons in the ways of Hasidism, and none of them knows the language of the land or secular knowledge; but his daughter often speaks only Polish.'" Dynner, *The Light of Learning*, 22–23.

22 See Glenn Dynner, "Hasidism and Habitat," in Dynner, ed., *Holy Dissent: Jewish and Christian Mystics in Eastern Europe* (Detroit, MI: Wayne State University Press, 2011), at 110. To some extent, narrator, author, and protagonist all seem to share the same perspective in this chapter: "For Hasidim who lived in modern cities, courts located in small towns were a repository of the premodern world that they had left behind, suffused in their imagination with the mystical atmosphere and moral values of tradition." Wodziński, *Hasidism: Key Questions*, 262.

GLOSSARY

Aliyah: Here, summons to recite blessings before and after the ritual reading of a section of the day's Torah portion

Azamer beshvokhin: "I will sing in praises," Shabbos evening hymn attributed to Rabbi Isaac Luria

Bloch, Jan (1836–1902): Convert to Christianity who was extremely successful in business and remained concerned with the welfare of the Jewish community

El Adon: Shabbos morning hymn focusing on the glories of Divine creation

Esrogim: Citrons used for the holiday of Sukkes

Eyn Yankev: Anthology of narrative material from the Babylonian Talmud

Farfel: Tiny pasta balls

Havdole: Ritual text and blessings formally marking the end of Shabbos

Kaboles shabes: Collection of Psalms and other texts intended to welcome the incoming Shabbos

Kalibyaler: Follower of Rebbe of Kołbiel (southeast of Warsaw), most likely Yoshua Asher Elhanan Ashkenazi, great-grandson of the Holy Jew of Przysucha

Kli Yoker: Torah commentary by Rabbi Shlomo Ephraim ben Aaron Luntschitz (1602)

Kreplekh: Soup dumplings, usually meat-filled, eaten especially on certain holidays including Purim

Kreysi uPleysi: Commentary on the Yoreh Deah section of the Shulchan Aruch by Rabbi Yonatan Eibeschütz (1763)

Lekha Dodi: Culminating hymn of the Kabbalat Shabbat service on Friday evening

Lulavim: Palm branches included as part of the Sukkes ritual

Maariv: Evening prayers

Maftir: Repeated reading of the last verses of the Torah portion for any given day

Maggid of Kozhenits: Yisroel Hopshtein (1737–1814), disciple of Reb Dov Ber of Mezritsh

Makhtsis-hashekel: Literally "half-shekel"; standardized donation to charity before the Purim holiday

Maos khitin: Literally "coins for wheat"; donation to provide Passover food for the needy

Mazones: Here, blessing recited over food made from various grains

Minchah: Afternoon prayers

Mordkhe Yosef Izhbitser: Leiner, disciple of Reb Simcha Bunem and of the Kotsker Reb Menachem Mendl Morgenstern, with whom he had a decisive break around 1840

Midrash Rabbah: Collection of midrashic texts on the Five Books and various other parts of the Hebrew Bible

Misnagdim: Opponents of Hasidism

Moshe Montefiore (1784–1885): British financier and banker, activist, philanthropist and Sheriff of London, of Sephardi background

Nokhem of Chernobl (1730–1798): Student of the Baal Shem Tov and of Dov Ber of Mezritsh

Oheyv Yisroel: Hasidic text by Avrohom Yehoshua Heshel (1748–1825)

Or HaChaim: Torah commentary by Rabbi Chaim ibn Attar (1696–1742)

Peyes: Long sidelocks worn by some male Jews in observance of the commandment not to cut the "corners" of the head

Pri Megodim: Supercommentary on two parts of Shulchan Aruch (Orach Chaim and Yoreh Deah), by Rabbi Joseph ben Meir Teumim (1782)

Radzimin: A far suburb of Warsaw. At the time this book takes place, the Radziminer Rebbe was Aharon Menachem Mendel Guterman

Ramosoyim Tsofim: Hasidic commentary on Tana D'Vey Eliyahu, composed by Rabbi Shmuel of Sieniawa (first published 1881)

Rizhiner: Probably Yisroel Friedman of Ruzhin (1796–1850), great-grandson of Dov Ber of Mezritsh

Rothschild, Meir Anshl (1744–1812): Founder of the Rothschild banking dynasty

Seer of Lublin (Ashkenazi Hebrew: Khoyze): Yaakov Yitzchak HaLevi Horowitz, active around the turn of the nineteenth century

Shabbos Hagadol: Literally the "Big" or "Great Shabbos," immediately preceding Passover; one of the two times each year a rabbi was traditionally expected to speak in shul

Shehakol: General blessing recited before consumption of certain foods or drinks

Sheygets: Derogatory term for a non-Jew, although here addressed to a Jew

Shkhine: The feminine Divine presence

Shlakhmones: Ritual giving of portions of food in celebration of the Purim holiday

Shney Lukhos Habris: Seventeenth-century compendium of ethics, mysticism, and law composed by Rabbi Isaiah HaLevi Horowitz

Sholem-Aleykhem: Hymn recited at the Shabbos table before Friday night dinner

Shoykhen Ad: "Who abides forever" (opening words of Shabbos morning service)

Shulchan Aruch: Compendium of Jewish law composed by Rabbi Joseph Karo and considered authoritative for centuries (first published 1565)

BIBLIOGRAPHY

Bacon, Gershon. *The Politics of Tradition: Agudat Yisrael in Poland, 1916–1939* (Jerusalem: Magnes Press, 1996).

Biale, David, David Assaf, Benjamin Brown, Uriel Gellman, Samuel C. Heilman, Moshe Rosman, Gadi Sagiv, and Marcin Wodziński. *Hasidism: A New History* (Princeton, NJ: Princeton University Press, 2018).

Boyarin, Jonathan. *A Storyteller's Worlds: The Education of Shlomo Noble in Europe and America* (New York: Holmes & Meir, 1994).

Dynner, Glenn. *Men of Silk* (New York: Oxford University Press, 2006).

Dynner, Glenn. "Hasidism and Habitat," in *Holy Dissent: Jewish and Christian Mystics in Eastern Europe*, ed. Glenn Dynner (Detroit, MI: Wayne State University Press, 2011).

Dynner, Glenn. *The Light of Learning: Hasidism in Poland on the Eve of the Holocaust* (New York: Oxford University Press, 2023).

Feierstein, Morris M. "Aleksander Hasidic Dynasty," in YIVO Encyclopedia of Jewish Eastern Europe at https://encyclopedia.yivo.org/article/184

Hartman, Saidiya. "Venus in Two Acts," *Small Axe: A Journal of Caribbean Criticism*, Vol. 12, No. 2 (June 2008), 1–14.

Heschel, Abraham Joshua. *A Passion for Truth* (New York: Farrar, Straus & Giroux, 1973).

Polonsky, Antony. YIVO Encyclopedia of Jews in Eastern Europe, s.v. "Warsaw" at https://encyclopedia.yivo.org/article/487

Rabinowicz, Tzvi M., ed. *The Encyclopedia of Hasidism* (Northvale, NJ: Jason Aronson, 1996), s.v. "Warsaw."

Toreck, Wojciech. "Mystic, Teacher, Troublemaker: Shimon Engel Horovits of Żelechòw and the Challenges of Hasidic Education in Interwar Poland," *Jewish Quarterly Review*, Vol. 110, No. 2 (Spring 2020), 313–342.

Tsaytlin, Aren. *Literarishe un filosofishe eseyen* (New York: Congress for Jewish Culture, 1980).

Wiesel, Elie. *Souls on Fire: Portraits and Legends of Hasidic Masters* (New York: Random House, 1972).

Wodziński, Marcin. *Hasidism and Politics: The Kingdom of Poland, 1815–1864* (Portland, OR: The Littman Library of Jewish Civilization, 2013).

Wodziński, Marcin. *Hasidism: Key Questions* (New York: Oxford University Press, 2018).

Wodziński, Marcin. *Historical Atlas of Hasidism* (Princeton, NJ: Princeton University Press, 2018).